Growing
from
Good
to
Great

**Positioning your
fund-raising efforts
for BIG gains**

Growing
from
Good
to
Great

Positioning your fund-raising efforts for BIG gains

Judith E. Nichols, Ph.D.,CFRE

Bonus Books, Inc., Chicago

© 1995 by Bonus Books, Inc.

99   98   97   96   95   5   4   3   2   1

Library of Congress Catalog Card Number: 95-75639
International Standard Book Number: 1-56625-035-8

Bonus Books, Inc.
160 East Illinois Street
Chicago, Illinois 60611

Cover design by Laura Reyes with Shane R. McCall

Printed in the United States of America

Contents

Introduction

Every day the demands made on our organizations increase. As government pulls back, charities are expected to fill the void. The leadership of every not-for-profit—religious, educational, health, human services, the arts, environmental, public/society benefit, and international affairs—in turn looks to its development team for relief. The mantra is always the same: "We need more money."

How much more money do our organizations need? Often, much more than the 5, 10, 15, or even 25% increases we've been struggling to raise each year. Every organization is caught in the same bind. The needs are real and urgent. But, too often, fund raisers are asked to be magicians: pulling miraculous gains out of an already overworked staff, volunteer pool, and budget.

What can we do?

> **It takes all the running you can do, to keep in the same place.**
>
> **If you want to get somewhere else, you must run twice as fast.**
>
> —Lewis Carroll, *Alice in Wonderland*

Growing from Good to Great: Positioning Your Fund-Raising Efforts for BIG Gains confronts this dilemma. My purpose is to help you logically reorganize your development strategy and fund-raising methodologies to support your efforts to move rapidly past the 5 to 25% benchmarks of growth to truly significant gains.

This reorganization need not add costs to your budget. Most not-for-profits actually spend *too much* given the results they achieve in their fund raising! *As you become more efficient and effective in your development efforts, the cost of raising money decreases.*

Growing from Good to Great: Positioning Your Fund-Raising Efforts for BIG Gains is intended to help you rethink how you organize your development program in light of a changing world. It will enable those new to fund raising or to their positions to move their development programs rapidly from the start. It will encourage more experienced fund raisers and those working with mature programs to rethink the linchpins of development philosophy.

Driving all my work is a common set of fund-raising truths:

To raise money effectively and efficiently you must:

- know who your current donors are;

- know who your best prospects might be;

- know how to evaluate the potential for fund raising from various development strategies and choose your priorities accordingly;

- know how to ask for money;

- know how much money to ask for.

SOURCE: *Targeted Fund-Raising: Defining and Refining Your Development Strategy,* Judith E. Nichols, Precept Press, 1991

To grow from good to great, you need to address each of these five truths in the unique way that best fits your organization.

Growing from Good to Great builds on the theories proposed in my earlier books, *Changing Demographics: Fund Raising in the 1990s, Targeted Fund Raising: Defining and Refining Your Development Strategy,* and *Pinpointing Affluence: Increasing Your Share of Major Donor Dollars.* While *Growing from Good to Great* is intended as a stand-alone "read," several of its underlying assumptions are expanded upon in previous books. Rather than repeat this material in depth, I have chosen to use it as a point of departure. For more detail, you may find consulting one or more of my previous books useful.

No book is written by the author alone. In the case of *Growing from Good to Great,* I owe a great debt to my colleagues who patiently let me try my theories on their organizations even as I was struggling to place them in a structure that made sense. There are so many people and organizations to thank that I could not list them all, but I'd like especially to acknowledge those I worked with most closely during the time this book took shape: Wende Wilson at the Columbia River Girl Scouts; Jim Minehart at United Church Homes; Jim Pfluger at the American Quarter Horse Association; and Astrid Berg at the American Lung Association of Washington, whose organizations acted as "living laboratories" for much of this work.

I'd like to add a very special thank you to my colleagues who made time in their very busy schedules to review the manuscript: Karen Sendelback, American Lung Association of Washington; Jim Minehart, United Church Homes; and Elaine Rhodes, Penn State University; provided valuable counsel and advice.

Judith E. Nichols, Ph.D., CFRE

PART ONE

Understanding Changing Paradigms: Are You Positioned for the Twenty-first Century?

> **To effectively raise money, you must understand how the world is changing.**

David Paradine, the recently-retired CEO of the United Way of Columbia-Willamette, Oregon, notes that "Change is not negotiable. It's inevitable." In fact, the Chinese proverb and curse—"May you live in interesting times"—is especially apropos given the tumultuous changes that are happening all around us. *The one thing we know with certainty about the future is that it's likely to be different from the present.*

Change presents both opportunities and challenges. While it can be threatening, disruptive, and anxiety-provoking, change is also transforming, revitalizing, and a source of energy. *Unfortunately, too often, change takes us unaware.* Then, we play "catch up": trying desperately to move to the new reality.

Simon George, director of development at the Good Shepherd Trust, Great Britain, suggests this test to check your response to change. Does your organization

- predict change and move ahead of it?

- recognize things have changed and manage to catch up?

- not even notice that change has occurred?

Notes Simon, "No prizes for guessing which will survive to meet tomorrow's needs!"

Let's introduce a term: paradigms. We live our lives based on paradigms. Paradigms are the assumptions that help establish boundaries. They provide us with

- rules for success;
- a filter for incoming experiences and data so that we can accept what fits and ignore the rest.

Paradigms are both common and useful. However, when you develop a terminal case of certainty you wind up with "paradigm paralysis."

To thrive, not just survive, you need to understand the changing population paradigms. And, you must be prepared to act on those changes. Futurist Joel Barker notes, "when the paradigm shifts, everyone goes back to zero." Your past successes no longer count . . . they guarantee you nothing! In fact, your successful past can block your vision of the future.

What are the changing population paradigms that fund raisers must understand to succeed in the years ahead?

Changing Population Paradigms

Increasing Longevity

- People are living longer
- Boomers are no longer babies
- The elderly are increasingly female

Increasing Diversity

- Generational differences
- Ethnic/racial pluralism
- Lifestage and lifestyle differences

When we look at our own profession, too many fund raisers are still working under the old rules: assuming an unlimited pool of donors to be acquired, treating everyone as if they share common "generational anchors," and clinging to methodologies that today's savvy consumers are rejecting.

Chapter One, "Changing Audiences," provides an overview of the most significant trends in population—increasing longevity and increasing diversity. Because the *who* has changed, the *how* must change.

Chapter Two, "Changing Technologies, Changing Methodologies," discusses how methods of communication are rapidly changing to fit the demands of our very different population.

Chapter Three, "Changing Fund-Raising Strategies," reminds us that our delivery of fund-raising appeals must fit our audiences. It puts the pieces together, suggesting the new, better approaches to today's—and tomorrow's—donors.

Because the *who* and the *how* have changed, fund raising must change as well.

CHAPTER ONE

Changing Audiences

A Population Overview through 2020

Between 1990 and 2020, the under-50 population is projected to grow by only 1%.

- **Fewer young adults:**
  By 1995, there will be 20% fewer 18- to 24-year-olds (nearly 5 million fewer prospects than there were in 1988).

***But** the 50-plus population is projected to grow by 74%.*

- **An older population:**
  In 1989, the majority of U.S. adults were over age 40. By 2002, the majority of U.S. adults will be over age 50. 63 million people alive today have celebrated their 50th birthday—34% of the entire adult population.

- **The fastest growing segments are boomers:**
  50- to 54-year-olds, followed by 45- to 49-year-olds, followed by those 55 to 59.

- **Increasing numbers of the elderly are female:**
  60% of the 65-and-over population are women, and because women usually live longer, women outnumber men *nearly 3 to 1* past age 85.

SOURCE: *Marketing to Boomers and Beyond: Strategies for Reaching America's Wealthiest Market*, David B. Wolfe, McGraw Hill, 1993

What are the changing population paradigms that fund raisers must understand to succeed in the years ahead? They fall into two general areas:

- Increasing longevity
- Increasing diversity

Increasing Longevity

- People are living longer
- Boomers are no longer "babies"
- The elderly are increasingly female

Increasing Longevity: Between 1990 and 2020, the under-50 population is projected to grow by only 1%, but the 50-plus population is projected to grow by 74%.

By 1995, there will be 20% fewer 18- to 24-year-olds (nearly 5 million fewer young adults) than there were in 1988. In 1989, thanks to the middle aging of the 76 million-plus Baby Boomers born from 1946 to 1964, the majority of U.S. adults were over age 40.

Medical advances have lengthened life expectancy in the U.S. from 45 years in 1900 to over 90 years today. With the huge Baby Boom population approaching their 50s, by 2002 the majority of American adults will be over age 50.

And increasingly, because women live an average of 7 years longer than men, the elderly will be female. Women outnumber men nearly 3 to 1 past age 85. Older women are also increasingly single. There are 14 million single women older than 55, compared to only 4 million single men. Moreover, most women marry older men. As a result, nearly half of elderly women are widowed, compared with just 14% of elderly men. *"The land of the old will be a land of women."*

Increasing Diversity

- Distinct generational differences
- Growing ethnic/racial pluralism
- Lifestage and lifestyle differences

Increasing Diversity: No longer will our best prospects be similar to one another. We will deal with diversity between age groups, lifestyles, and ethnic/racial backgrounds.

As life expectancy lengthens, there will be more differences among age groups. Our "generational anchors" will not be the same: We have different points of reference and different childhood experiences. Today, there are more Americans who were born after World War II than ever before:

- Eighty-five percent of Americans are not old enough to remember the 1929 stock market crash

- Seventy percent don't remember "before television"

- Sixty-six percent are not old enough to remember the Korean War

- Fifty percent are not old enough to remember the assassination of John F. Kennedy

Different life experiences mean that fund raisers and prospects may lack common life "triggers." Our philanthropic personalities and our attitudes towards money will not be the same. Fund raisers will need to do more "intergenerational" selling.

Each generation has its own personality. Projecting the cycle is a new way of predicting consumer attitudes and lifestyles. Historians William Strauss and Neil Howe suggest we can read behavior along a "generational diagonal." There are four "generational personalities"—idealistic, reactive, civic, and adaptive—which recur in that order throughout history. According to Strauss and Howe, "To understand the differences between generations, ask how they were raised as children, what public events they witnessed in adolescence, and what social mission elders gave them as they came of age."

To succeed in reaching all of these generations, your messages will have to pay attention not to where a cohort has been, but rather to where it is headed. (The terms "cohort" and "generation," though often used interchangeably, are not exactly the same. A generation is usually defined by its years of birth. Cohorts are better defined by events that occur at various critical points in the group's lifetime.)

To make this information useful for fund raisers, I have sifted through a number of demographic and psychographic theories concerning cohorts. I've combined the oldest groupings together, as the numbers are extremely small, and concluded that there are five age groups we will deal with. As America moves into the twenty-first century, our prime audiences will be:

- **Depression Babies:** the 32 million Americans born prior to 1939 have "civic" personalities—believing it is the role of the citizen to fit into society and make it better. Always mindful of the lessons of their childhood, their money personalities are conservative. They are the donors we have become used to serving: willing to take direction, "traditional," seeing volunteerism and philanthropy as their duty.

- **World War II Babies:** born from 1940 to 1945, this smaller group of 16 million Americans was taught to be "silent," believing in the will of the group rather than individuality. Their parents drilled the lessons of the Great Depression into them but they reached adulthood in golden economic days, benefitting from real estate appreciation, a booming stock market, portable pensions, government entitlements, and inflation. Now in early retirement, many are willing to spend on themselves if not on charity.

  "The Eisenhower Generation" (Silents) will respond to appeals to their other-directed pluralism, trust in expertise, emulation of the young, and unquenched thirst for adventure. Preferred message style: sensitive and personal, with an appeal to technical detail.

  Both Depression and World War II Babies tend to be cash payers, distrusting newer technologies. They tend to listen to society's recommendations and like to support traditional charities such as United Way.

- **Baby Boomers:** America's 78 million "idealists" (76 million born in the U.S. from 1946 to 1964 and 2 million immigrants) have been hard for society to swallow. Taught from birth that they were special, Boomers believe in changing the world, not changing to fit it. Having always lived in a society of inflation and having no memories of the Depression, they have a different understanding of money. They tend to buy first, pay later and like monthly payment plans and using credit cards. While pre- and World War II Americans tend to believe that $25 is a meaningful gift, Boomers and younger adults believe it takes $100.

"Boom midlifers" (unlike "Silent midlifers") will see virtue in austerity and a well-ordered inner life. Also, they will demand a new assertion of community values over individual wants. Preferred message style: meditative and principled, with an undertone of pessimism.

- **Baby Busters:** the 33 million "reactive" Americans born from 1965 to 1977 are the first generation of Americans to distrust the American Dream. They don't believe life will be better for them than their parents' and see their role in life as pragmatic. They want to fix rather than change. Still being supported in adulthood by parents, many have high discretionary income that they will give to charities they work with. Highly computer literate, they prefer the cashless society.

  "Generation X" (unlike Boomer adults) will need convincing proof that your organization is reliable and will simplify rather than complicate their lives. Preferred message style: blunt and kinetic, with an appeal to brash survivalism.

- **Baby Boomlet:** the 45 million-plus "civic" children of Boomers, born from 1978 through 1996, hold many of the values of an earlier generation. They are growing up in a world without boundaries and are likely to extend their philanthropy well past their own country.

  Unlike their Buster brothers and sisters, the "Millennium Generation" will believe in science and co-operation, and will be easily persuaded that theirs is a good and special group that knows how to build big things together. Preferred message style: rational and constructive, with an undertone of optimism.

  Younger Americans are likely to look for more "personal" charities and to dislike workplace giving. They are more participatory in personality style; supporting only the organizations they actively work with.

Complicating the need to segment the differences between age groups, we will need to factor in differences in lifestyles and lifestages. A growing number of adults are moving through life at their own pace: postponing or not having children, taking sabbaticals from careers, returning to school, starting new businesses, etc. Remarriage, second families, and caregiving change the way adults of similar ages look at their ability to be charitable.

Only 34% of American households currently have children under 18 living at home.

- Couples without children are not by any means all "young marrieds": The majority are 35 and over. And almost 4 in 10 are "empty nesters," a group that includes someone 50 to 64.

- The proportion of married persons among U.S. adults declined from 72 to 61% between 1970 and 1991, according to the U.S. Census. The nation's 41 million never-marrieds represent one of the fastest-growing segments of the adult population, nearly doubling in the last 20 years.

- The number of women age 35 to 54 who live alone should increase from 2.6 million in 1990 to 3.4 million in 2000. That's a 30% rise for the Boomer years, compared to 24% for all women living alone.

We will also be dealing with an increasingly culturally and ethnically diverse base of prospects.

Not-for-profits need to learn how to be inclusive with diverse client populations, volunteers, boards, and donors. Minorities will exert more influence over the national agenda as the population of African Americans, Hispanics, and Asian Americans increases from 17% in 1990 to 33% by 2000. In 1990, 1 out of 6 workers belonged to an ethnic minority. By 2000, they will be 1 in 3.

In 1995, 63% of births will be to non-Hispanic white women. By 2050, the share could decrease to 41%. Blacks and Native

Americans will only slightly increase their share of births. The share of Asian American births will increase from 4 to 9% by 2050, while the share of Hispanic-origin births will rise from 16 to 29%. By the year 2010, 1 in 3 children will be either non-white or Hispanic.

In the past two decades, the Hispanic population in America more than doubled. This growth is projected to continue: rising from 24 million in 1992 to 31 million by the year 2000, and on to 81 million by 2050. After 1996, the Hispanic population is projected to add over 870,000 people to the nation's population each year. This is more than any other racial or ethnic group. By 2010, the Hispanic origin population may become the second-largest ethnic group in the U.S.

Asian and Native Americans will be the fastest-growing segment of the work force, increasing 81% in 13 years. They will be followed by Hispanics of all races, with a projected growth of 64%. The number of blacks in the labor force should increase 25%, and the number of non-Hispanic whites should grow 11%. However, the sheer number of non-Hispanic whites mean that they will continue to dominate the labor force through 2005, with their share diminishing only slightly from 78% in 1992 to 73% in 2005.

Minority Markets in the U.S.

Issue	African American	Asian American	Hispanic American
Market Size and Growth	Largest racial minority	Fastest-growing minority	Projected largest minority by 2015?
Regional Stronghold	South, MSAs,* central cities	West Coast (CA)	CA; FL, TX, NY
Demographic Sketch	Young families, many female heads of households	Family-oriented	High birth rates, male dominant, extended families
Socioeconomic Sketch	Lower income, less education (generally)	High income, well-educated, entrepreneurs	Income varies by subgroup
Marketing Implications	Strong middle class emerging, twofold media (general and black)	Influenced by Eastern cultures, savers, loyal customers	Spanish-language media, quality seekers

Especially because target audiences span several generations, you need to vary how you communicate with them and understand the changing paradigms of technology. This is the focus of chapter two.

---

*Metropolitan Statistical Areas

CHAPTER TWO

Changing Technologies,
Changing Methodologies

The New Marketing Paradigm

"Technology is transforming choice,
and choice is transforming the marketplace."

SOURCE: "Marketing Is Everything," Regis McKenna, *Harvard Business Review,* Jan/Feb
1991

OUR SOCIETY IS **in a perpetual state of change, notes Regis
McKenna.** Everything is changing . . . companies change, industries
change, products change, distribution channels change, issues change.
Alvin Toffler put this in perspective when he suggested we look at
long-term economic waves. The first two, the shift from hunting-gath-
ering to agriculture and from agriculture to the industrial age, are completed. We are now in the third wave, moving from the industrial age
to the age of information.

Over the next 20 years, many experts believe that the information
technology may change more than it has over the last 200 years because

- everyone wants to know more about everything;

- people need more information, faster.

**Today, you can have your own version of virtually any prod-
uct.** Not-for-profits and their fund-raising methodologies will need to
change in response.

Don Peppers and Martha Rogers, writing in *The One to One*

Future: Building Relationships One Customer at a Time, caution that "The old paradigm, a system of mass production, mass media, and mass marketing, is being replaced by a totally new paradigm, a one-to-one economic system." Economies of scale will never again be as important as they are today.

An article in the *Boston Globe,* "The Narrowing of America," by Chris Reidy, noted by E. Janice Leeming and Cynthia F. Tripp in *Segmenting the Women's Market*, perhaps sums it up best: "Once each city had a single radio station, and Americans all sang the same songs of love. Ice cream came in three flavors. Everyone seemed to drive a Ford or Chevy. And the Crayola box held a mere eight crayons. . . . That's all changed, of course. . . . Life in the '90s is a glorious boutique of options. As choice proliferates, vanilla and white bread become colors of contempt, the invention of new flavors and new colors creates a boom industry. In the latest Crayola box, periwinkle is but one of 96 choices."

John Gorman, senior vice president of Epsilon, agrees that the increasingly affordable economics of communication and technology is driving this technological shift:

- less direct mail because of its high cost

- increasing flexibility of the printed medium

- availability of interactive media

Mal Warwick, writing in *Technology and the Future of Fundraising*, predicts that "the business of direct-mail fund raising is changing in genuinely fundamental ways under the onslaught of new technologies—inter-networking, 'multimedia,' wireless communications, etc. Our appeals will need to be individualized, multi-sensory, information-rich, immediate, interactive, and communal."

The new commandment of Information-Age Marketing: "Tell, tell, tell, before you start to sell, sell, sell." Baby Boomers have been called "information junkies." They want specific information on the issues that interest them. However, they are too sophisticated to respond to intense, emotional appeals.

Low-key "telling" is going to increasingly replace high-pressure "selling" as the most effective way to get through to jaded consumers as we move further along in the shift from mass marketing to individualized marketing.

Your Message is Competing with Information Overload:

- 62% of homes have cable television, with an average of 51 channels per home

- There are over 2,400 consumer magazine titles

- Over 30 million homes have a personal computer

- Over 70% of individuals have shopped by phone or mail

- *Time* magazine now produces over 100 versions each week

- There are over 20 different interactive systems in various stages of testing

SOURCE: *Beyond 2000: The Future of Direct Marketing*, Jerry I. Reitman, NTC Business Books, 1994

Today's mid-life American (the Baby Boom generation born between 1946 to 1964) has its own informational and financial profile. Raised in the era of television, Boomers are impatient with slower methods of receiving information and suspicious of direct mail as well. Videos (rarely used by not-for-profits) are a good way of breaking through the media "clutter." Boomers prefer face-to-face and phone conversations. As they accept that their life span is likely to take them well into their 90s, few will make major gifts from assets. Major gift giving will take place by bequest instead. To pay for gifts: time payments—just like they pay for everything else—is the preferred methodology.

An emerging communication tool is the infomercial, the long versions of television advertising. Ninety percent of consumers with household incomes of more than $50,000 a year are most likely to be aware of infomercials. Eighty-four percent (compared with 74% of those with incomes of $30,000 to $50,000, and 61% of those with incomes below $30,000) have viewed at least 5 minutes of one of these programs. To use infomercials effectively, your organization needs to choose a schedule that encourages multiple viewing. Almost three-quarters of those who made a purchase (73%) watched the infomercial more than once. Only 27% were sold after the first viewing. Nearly 7 in 10 (69%) are female. More than half of those who purchase from infomercials watch 1 to 4 ads a week.

America's ready for the Digital Fast Lane. More than one-quarter (27%) of American adults own personal computers and another 10% plan to purchase one within the next 6 months. Of those who already own a PC, nearly half (49%) also own a modem and another 11% plan to buy one in the next 6 months. On-line services (e.g., Prodigy, CompuServe) have experienced huge growth in recent years; 14% of PC owners are members of an on-line service, and 13% plan on becoming a member within the next 6 months.

Because younger audiences prefer it, an increased use of electronic newsletters, videos, e-mail and computer bulletin boards should be in your organization's future. Already 1.3 million Americans have used Prodigy for philanthropy. The computer network program allows people to look at information about the economic status of young children, take a brief quiz, and send for information on charities that work with children.

The Chronicle of Philanthropy reported on the Internet NonProfit Center, which is run entirely by volunteers. The Center was set up by Buster Cliff Landesman, a graduate student at Princeton University to make it "faster, cheaper, and easier" for donors to learn about charities. Using the Center, you can peruse the "Best Buys for Big Hearts" list of the top charities in various categories, such as the environment or youth, as ranked by the American Institute of Philanthropy, a watchdog organization based in St. Louis. The institute bases its ranking on the percentage of a group's income that goes to charitable programs. You can also retrieve a Donor's Defense Kit that includes tips on "how to say 'no' without guilt," electronic versions of charity annual reports, and suggestions about how to obtain more information on charities.

Other "roadmaps" are springing up to help potential donors navigate the Internet:

> • Ellen Spertus, a Massachusetts Institute of Technology graduate student now at Microsoft Corporation, first helped the Global Fund for Women. She then set up a list of not-for-profit information sites which runs on software using the World Wide Web technology. With a few clicks of a computer mouse, reports *The Chronicle*, people can

be connected to the Internet site that has the information they want.

- ReliefNet is a new network that provides information on international relief efforts, offers users a way to make a pledge electronically to the group(s) of their choice, and serves as a link to other information about relief efforts posted on the Internet. Jack Hidary, director of EarthWeb and creator of the ReliefNet, notes that most donors to relief groups tend to be over 40: "ReliefNet is a means of conveying to another generation the work that's being done."

Marketing on the Internet: How it is different from other media

- You can't talk at the user but must, rather, talk *with* the user. Interact with the user whenever possible. Involve him or her in the marketing message and give the user the illusion of control.

- Make your message interesting. Educate and entertain the user with lively copy and graphics when appropriate. Change portions of the marketing message frequently to keep your presence fresh and inviting.

- Support and promote your commercial Internet presence. Index your location in Internet directories and use traditional communications and public relations practices to inform the public of your off-line location.

- You must make information available with a means for response.

SOURCE: "The Basics of Marketing on the Internet," Jay Christensen, *DM News*, December 5, 1994

Learn to use technology. Stop fighting the inevitable! Marketing, notes *Business Week*, has moved well past mass marketing (when a vast, undifferentiated body of prospects received identical, mass-produced messages). It's even moved past market segmentation (which divides still-anonymous consumers into smaller groups with common demographic or psychographic characteristics). Now, new generations of faster, more powerful computers are enabling marketers to zero in on ever-smaller niches of the population, ultimately aiming for the smallest consumer segment of all: the individual.

The paradigms are changing and we must change with them. As we move into the new century you will need to segment not only your prospect audiences, but also your fund-raising methodologies and your fulfillment options. The key to the future is delivering the information and accepting gift fulfillment in *whatever* format your donor prefers.

There is a major paradigm shift around financial technology: *Americans are letting go of checks and cash.* Eighteen percent—up 200% since 1986—use cards and computers to pay bills, including gifts to charity. This is good news for not-for-profits: it is looking at the checkbook balance that keeps gift amounts low! Few of us are comfortable writing a single, large check for charity. Not because we don't care, but rather because we think we can't afford the gesture.

- *Both Depression and World War II Babies tend to be cash payers, distrusting new technologies.* These are the generations that still "tuck" emergency cash into wallets and handbags. Many prefer a "hands-on" arrangement with bill paying and are uncomfortable using ATMs and other modern technologies. They are most likely to choose one-time check writing. To them, major gift giving means selling or giving away an asset: solid, real gifts.

   Depression and World War II Babies tend to listen to society's recommendations and like to support traditional, well-established charities. Your mature donors will continue to prefer traditional methods of fund raising and fulfillment. Those over 50 are the most literate of Americans and actually enjoy receiving well-done direct mail.

- *Boomers and younger persons grew up in a different world.* They tend to prefer the "cashless society," using credit cards, standing bank drafts, and electronic transfers. Younger donors are the heaviest users of debit cards. According to a Gallup Organization survey: nearly one-quarter (24%) of people age 18 to 23 have debit cards, as do 22% of those age 35 to 54; only 12% of respondents age 55 or over have them.

Boomers are making it clear they distrust workplace giving and have given rise to a whole generation of new charities: more personal in nature than those their parents and grandparents founded and supported. Baby Busters are quite philanthropic but see themselves as having only small amounts of disposable cash to give to charity. (Rather, their priorities include sharing with a large extended family of friends and colleagues.) Their gift fulfillment needs to be structured to allow for a constant stream of extremely modest gift amounts.

The marketing matrix for methodologies and fulfillment will look somewhat like this:

Audience	Fund-Raising Methodology	Fulfillment Option
Mature Donors (50 years and older)	Face-to-face, Direct mail	Checks or one-time gifts of assets made during lifetime via planned giving, as well as bequests
Mid-Aged Donors (30 to 50 years)	Face-to-face, Telephone	Pledges over time and one-time gifts via credit cards; major gifts via bequest only
Younger Donors (18 to 30 years)	Computer network	Continuous gifts via electronic fund transfer and bank draft; use of debit cards rather than credit cards; little hope of major gifts

Not-for-profits and charities have lagged far behind businesses in understanding how the changes in our population and the changes in technology have lead our donors and prospects to expect different methodologies. In the next chapter we'll explore how to place this information in a strategic framework.

CHAPTER THREE

Changing Fund-Raising Strategies

> **When the paradigm shifts,
> everyone goes back to zero.**
>
> **Because the *who* has changed,
> the *how* must change as well.**

THE INCREASING LONGEVITY and diversity of our population changes its response to technology and, in turn, will change the way we do fund raising in fundamental ways. Different life experiences mean that our donors and prospects will lack common life "triggers." Their philanthropic personalities and attitudes towards money will not be the same. The differences will mean we will need to do more "intergenerational" marketing.

Too many of us still work under the old paradigms: assuming we can assess an unlimited pool of donors, treating all donors and prospects as if they share common "generational anchors," and ignoring changing—often preferred—methodologies and technologies for both marketing and fulfillment.

Because your donors and prospects are living longer:

- concentrate on renewal and upgrading donors rather than on the acquisition of new prospects;

- prepare to receive major-gift income through planned gifts and legacies rather than through current giving.

Because the majority of adults were born after World War II, not before:

- don't expect automatic donor loyalty; it comes only with involvement

- suggest meaningful levels of giving: $100 as opposed to $25 to "make a difference."

Let's look briefly at each changing paradigm in turn:

Because your donors and prospects are living longer:

- **Concentrate on renewal and upgrading donors rather than on the acquisition of new prospects.**

In the 1970s and 1980s there were always more and more new prospects. This was because, during those years, wave after wave of Baby Boomers reached adulthood. When the baby boom ended, so did the ever increasing pool of new prospects. *From the mid-1990s and beyond, we're dealing with a much smaller group of new adults for acquisition.* However, we get to deal with the same prospects over and over again. Length of life is increasing dramatically even as numbers of "new" adults are decreasing.

> **The median age of our population is moving past 40.**

In 1986, the first of the Baby Boomers turned 40. As the massive Boomer cohort of 78 million (76 million born in the U.S. plus 2 million immigrants) moved from young adulthood to middle age, it caused the traditional population pyramid to bulge in the middle.

During the 1950s to 1970s, we had a large number of children and teenagers, a medium number of young through 40s adults, and a very small grouping of mature adults and the elderly, forming the traditional population pyramid.

In the 1980s through 2000, the pyramid's Baby Boomers are moving into their adult years and, as a result, the population pyramid has "bulged" in the middle and become a rectangle.

And, because people can only get older, as we move into the twenty-first century, our rectangle becomes top-heavy with older individuals and the population pyramid inverts.

Fifty years from now, when middle-aging Baby Boomers join the ranks of the elderly, the old may outnumber the young. *If you don't work hard now to retain your best donors, you won't be able to replace them with new ones.*

The population is "bulging" in the middle and "tipping" towards the old. Between now and 2000:

- Births—reflecting the tail end of the baby boomlet—will decline slightly from 4 to 3.9 million annually through 2000.

- The Baby Boomlet—moving into the teen years—will reverse the decline in this age category (Baby Busters) seen between 1980 and 1994.

- Baby Busters—The pool of 25- to 34-year-olds—will decrease by 5.5 million.

- Late Boomers—The pool of 35- to 44-year-olds—will increase by 5.4 million.

- Early Boomers—the age grouping of 45- to 54-year-olds— today's 35- to 44-year-old Baby Boomers—will show the largest increase from 25.7 million to 37.1 million by the turn of the century.

- World War II Babies—The age grouping of 55- to 64-year-olds will grow from 21 to 24 million.

- Depression Year Babies—Those age 65 and over—will rise from 32 to 35 million.

SOURCE: *Population Projections of the United States, by Age, Sex, Race, and Hispanic Origin: 1993 to 2050,* Department of Commerce, U.S. Census Bureau, November 1993

As more and more people live longer and longer, their lifelong value to your organization grows as well. Because of their increasing longevity, donors you attract at age 40 will—with proper cultivation and donor relationship-building activities—continue to give, year after year at upgraded levels, for 30, 40, 50 or more years. Hopefully, your organization will receive the ultimate gift as well: a bequest.

To create this lifelong "bonding" will require that we thoroughly rethink the way we do business. For most not-for-profits the focus has been on acquisition of donors, not renewal. Flipping our philosophy to an aftermarketing focus requires a restructuring of resources, time, and values.

- **Prepare to receive major gift income through planned gifts and legacies rather than through current giving.**

The fastest growing age groups are the oldest ones. Of all the people who have lived to age 65 in the history of the world, more than half are alive today. The general U.S. elderly population grew 89% compared with total population growth of 39%. People age 85 and over have increased 232% since 1960. The 1990 census showed that 57,000 Americans have reached 100—a growth of 77% from the 1980 census. For every 100 women 85 years or over, there are just 39 men in the same age group. Almost one-third of the elderly, 28%, live alone.

> **The capital campaign of today will give way to the endowment campaign of tomorrow.**

It takes about 15 years for our perceptions to catch up with reality. Most of us are just beginning to understand the implications of our increasing longevity. Soon we will, and with that acceptance will come an understandable reluctance to part with assets that might be needed to sustain lifestyles and handle the threat of end-of-life medical needs.

You need to begin preparing for this logical resistance to current, sacrificial giving today. Because it typically takes 3 to 5 years for a planned-giving program to begin producing, it's especially important to put a strong program in place now.

Another thought: by creating a steady flow of bequests and

planned gifts, your organization will actually have a more stable income stream in the future.

Because the majority of adults were born after World War II, not before:

- **Don't expect automatic donor loyalty.**

While 89% of Americans give to charity every year, few have a single priority. The typical American donates to 11 to 14 charities each year and often cannot differentiate between one good organization in the field and another. In addition, options often exist for meeting the donor's needs, goals, and objectives in the world of business: *never before have our constituents faced so many choices.*

A key characteristic of Baby Boomers—the largest of our adult population groupings—is a growing alienation and falling confidence in leadership. *All their lives, Boomers have had to compete for resources and recognition.* As a result, they have grown up distrustful of institutions and unwilling to be taken for granted. Boomers and younger adults also tend to be less forgiving of poor service; less tolerant of mistakes and mismanagement by and within our organizations;

Behind Boomers' Growing Dissatisfaction

Much of the Boomers' skepticism and lack of loyalty has been developed or reinforced by their workplace experience. Among these:

- **The Fortune 500 effect:** move away from major companies with their stability and towards smaller, less "secure" employment

- **The death of lifetime employment:** the social contract between employer and employee has been broken

- **Raiders of the lost ARCO:** the need to survive has overtaken the desire to provide safe harbor, unless corporations can be persuaded that such loyalty to employees results in bottom-line results, long and short term

SOURCE: *Future Tense: The Business Realities of the Next Ten Years*, Ian Morrison and Greg Schmid, William Morrow & Co., 1994

and more impatient to have their concerns addressed promptly and properly.

Notes Jenny Thompson of Craver, Mathews, Smith: "American corporations—painfully and expensively—have finally come to understand the old concept of 'mass marketing'; 'customer loyalty' and 'brand loyalty' have gone the way of Pan American airlines, Macy's Department Store, Sears, and even venerable IBM. Consumers are now better informed . . . have access to far more information . . . are demanding more information . . . and show their loyalty only to those who provide good information and high-quality service."

With today's middle-aging and younger adults *there is no second chance.* You must deliver every time and constantly recultivate. You need to find ways to integrate the donor into your organization; to create and sustain a relationship that "bonds" customer to the not-for-profit.

- **suggest meaningful levels of giving: $100 as opposed to $25 to "make a difference."**

When it comes to making discretionary purchases, we all go back to our childhood memories of what money was worth. Charitable gifts—like leisure activities and the small luxuries of life (a splurge on chocolate or the purchase of the latest novel)—are often decided impulsively. Because they are not "must do" purchases (such as food, clothing, and shelter are considered), the purchaser must feel good about the expenditure.

> **Don't ask for too little.**

The majority of our adult population grew up in inflationary times. While pre- and World War II audiences tend to continue to believe that $25 is a meaningful level of giving, those born from 1946 on see $100 as having the same buying power.

Once you understand the broad strategic implications of changing demographics and technologies, your organization must adopt specific developmental plans that address the issues, concerns, and opportunities the new paradigms raise.

According to Ken Burnett, author of *Relationship Fundraising*, you will need to focus on:

- establishing comprehensive, useable donor histories;

- forming lasting relationships with donors;

- evaluating donors objectively;

- acquiring new donors at acceptable cost levels;

- developing an integrated approach to donor communication;

- segmenting donor files;

- giving donors choices;

- encouraging donors to give more, more regularly;

- making giving by bequest irresistible;

- adapting to new government requirements.

Each of these issues is addressed throughout *Growing from Good to Great*. Our starting point is to discuss how well, overall, your organization is positioned for requesting and attracting financial support. The issues of mission, advocates, and resources are highlighted in Part Two.

PART TWO

Do You Have the "Basics"?

You cannot ask for support unless three key elements are in place:

1. There must be a clear vision of what the organization is and wants to accomplish, with a menu of specific needs that support the mission.

2. There must be a dedicated and trained group of board members and volunteers committed to serving as its advocates in fund raising.

3. There must be commitment to providing the resources to carry out the strategy.

Only when all three elements are present can you create a realistic, yet challenging, development strategy—one that will encourage your organization to grow from good to great.

In order to maximize your fund-development efforts, you need to start by:

- evaluating what is currently being done;

- realistically assessing the potential for raising money from different audiences;

- choosing strategy steps and tools to best move you from where you are to where you need to be quickly and cost effectively, with sensitivity to your organization's culture and history.

In order to decide where you are, where you're going, and how you'll get there, your organization will need to carefully consider:

- How well thought out are our campaign needs?

- How committed is our board to achieving campaign success?

- Do we have a constituency base that is able and willing to respond to those needs?

- Do we have the resources needed to carry out campaign objectives successfully?

- How competent and prepared are our staff and volunteers?

- Where are we today and what are we selling to the public, to our donors?

- Is what we are today what we want to be tomorrow?

- Do our potential donors perceive us in the same manner we perceive ourselves?

- Do they, by and large, approve of our work and endorse our objectives for tomorrow?

- What kinds of financial resources will we need to finance the objectives we have in mind for tomorrow?

- What are our financial priorities in everything from construction to program funds?

- Are the people in our institution behind our vision and do they understand the goals ahead?

- With whom are we competing? Is there anything particularly unique or distinctive about our approach to the field?

- How do we best communicate our distinctions, goals, and objectives to our donors?

- Where do our board members and volunteers fit in?

- How do the roles of executive director, board members, development, and other staff and volunteers complement each other in the development process?*

Chapters four through six will help you to explore the basics: creating an organizational vision, building a strong group of board advocates, and structuring a development office that supports your fund raising.

---

*To decide on the specific strategic directions to take, I recommend conducting a development assessment. See chapters 20 and 21 of my book *Targeted Fund Raising: Defining and Refining Your Development Strategy* (Precept Press, 1991).

CHAPTER FOUR

Interpreting the Organizational Vision

It Starts with Mission

- Mission must be feasible, distinctive, and motivational
- There must be congruence between your mission and the marketplace and the marketplace's image of *you*

SOURCE: Growth Design Corporation

THE STARTING POINT is "organizational relevance." Does your organization have a mission that is valued in today's society?

Donors give for *their* needs, not yours. You can't raise money without a clearly-defined mission, a set of supporting goals and objectives, and a series of action steps to move you towards your target. In today's rapidly changing world this is no easy task.

The vital topic of organizational relevance is worthy of a book of its own. Many good ones are available and I urge you to use them in shaping your organization's vision of the future. For the purposes of this book, I will assume your organization *is* relevant. Our job in *Growing from Good to Great* is to look at how the organizational vision impacts on your ability to raise funds.

Once you've identified your organizational vision, you need to package it. According to Jody Hornor, author of *Power Marketing for Small Business*, you must position your not-for-profit to stand out from others serving your field. This can be done by using a unique selling proposition (USP) which takes the intent of your positioning strategy and translates it into a catchy phrase or slogan:

- Study your organization's features and benefits carefully to determine your uniqueness.

- Access your competition thoroughly to know what you are up against.

- Use your USP consistently in all communications with your donors.

Here is an example of a USP created for the Columbia River Girl Scout Council. It appears on all Council literature:

> The Columbia River Girl Scout Council supports 18,667 girls, young women, and adults in 43 Neighborhood Service Teams and 1,056 troops in 13 counties in Southwest Washington and Northwest Oregon along the Columbia River, covering 33,500 square miles. One girl in nine in our community belongs to Girl Scouting. We help these valuable young women to meet the growing responsibilities of our families, social institutions, communities, nation, and world through innovative programs which are educational and preventative in nature—and fun!

At the Columbia River Girl Scout Council, an expanded version of the USP appears on the back of every piece of development correspondence. Since it's on the back of the letterhead, it educates donors and prospects without the need for a separate brochure.

COLUMBIA RIVER GIRL SCOUT COUNCIL
A Major Community and Human Asset

Columbia River Girl Scouts is a major force in our community, providing a unique value-rooted, people-centered movement of exceptional, informal educational programs focusing on the interests and abilities of girls aged 5 to 17. As our girls reach out to explore their dreams and learn how to be their best, they truly honor our entire community.

Columbia River Girl Scout Council encompasses 18,667 girls and adults in 43 Neighborhood Service Teams and 1,056 troops in 13 counties in Southwest Washington and Northwest Oregon along the Columbia

(continued)

River, covering 33,500 square miles. *One girl in nine* (aged 5 to 17) *in our community belongs to the Council.* Girl scouting provides a diverse menu of membership and outreach programs that communicate values, serve the community, and enrich and educate the lives of participants.

Girl Scouting allows each girl the avenue in which to define her role in today's changing society and teaches her the skills to meet future challenges.

Under the guidance and direction of professionally trained staff and volunteer leaders, Girl Scout activities are designed to achieve four major program objectives:

1. To deepen awareness of oneself as a unique person of worth;

2. To relate to others with skill, maturity, and confidence;

3. To develop values that give meaning and direction to life;

4. To contribute to the betterment of society in a cooperative effort with others.

For 1994-95, Columbia River Girl Scout Council is committed to continue and expand upon its accomplishments:

• Program initiatives that address contemporary issues that build self-esteem and provide positive role models for girls in their formative years including math, science, and technology; health and fitness; and outdoor education.

• A commitment to bridging the barriers that keep us from serving and being served by a pluralistic society through customized programs to African-American, Hispanic, Native-American, and Asian-American girls and to abled and disabled youth.

• Over 75,000 hours of community service each year through recycling and environmental activities as well as providing food and shelter to the homeless and disadvantaged.

$110.04 supports one Girl Scout for one year.
One out of every nine girls (age 5-17) in your community is a
Columbia River Girl Scout.
Help us reach the other 120,000 girls who want to be Girls Scouts.

Not only do you need to educate your supporters and prospects as to why your organization is relevant today—and tomorrow—you need to translate for them what the costs will be to achieve your goals and objectives.

Organizations need different types of contributions to be raised for different needs. The first step in creating a long-range development strategy is always to define what must be raised and match that to the groups of donors most likely to have interest and ability in funding these needs.

The following are the most commonly identified needs:

Operating Needs—unrestricted funding for programs and services that are offered on an ongoing basis. Best served by gifts from donors who are willing to let you determine the "area of greatest need."
- Target Audience: Annual givers of all amounts

Capital Needs—restricted funding for specific projects or programs that arise as special, usually one-time, needs. Can include facility building and renovation, equipment purchase, and upgrading, etc.
- Target Audience: Major donors of $1,000 and more

Endowment Needs—unrestricted and restricted funding that creates a "safety net" for the organization. Typically recommended as the capital needed to produce 20% of the operating needs.
- Target Audience: Bequest and planned donors

I recommend involving everyone in your organizational "family" in defining the needs. A bottom-up, rather than a top-down, approach is essential. A simple way is to start with the operations staff and ask them to interpret their specific areas of responsibility into funding requests. Emphasize you want not only examples of current programs, projects, and services, but also what it would take to expand ongoing areas and create new delivery systems. The proposals are reviewed by mid- and upper-management and then presented to the board for its approval.

The results of this exercise are often startling. When the entire family reviews what will actually be needed to maintain and then expand the organizational vision, the perspective shifts.

Once completed, examples from the exercise can be used to provide donors and prospects with a narrative description of what gifts of all amounts accomplish. The finished brochure version is often called a "wish list," a full description of which is provided in Appendix A.

Articulating the cost of your organization's needs is a good first step to destroy an unspoken problem within your development family: the "Groucho syndrome."

Many not-for-profits need to start by shifting the perspective of their boards, staffs, and volunteers. Does your family secretly think your organization is too small or insignificant to catch the attention of donors? Chances are many of your family members have the Groucho syndrome—somehow thinking that "any organization that would have me as a (board, staff, or volunteer) member can't be that great."

Your family is working from a paradigm predicated on the Groucho syndrome. And, *until you shift their thinking*, they will continue to work from the old paradigm that argues "we aren't big enough, important enough, special enough, etc. to deserve additional funding."

The ramifications of the Groucho syndrome are:

- family members who do not serve as advocates of your organization. They are unable or unwilling to help the greater community know of your worth.

- family members who do not make their own contributions at a meaningful level. Your organization is not their priority.

- family members who do not ask others for money.

The Groucho syndrome is a serious problem and one that needs to be addressed carefully. There is no simple answer, but there is a process: committing to the continuing education of family members. The educational process begins with the formal orientation of all new family members. Regularly scheduled updates—both in meetings and in writing—need to be circulated.

I usually recommend confronting the Groucho syndrome head-on: holding a special family meeting in which this is discussed frankly and fully. Specific examples of your organization's successes and leadership must be provided at this time. Sharing with the family the organizational vision and its cost takes place at this gathering.

Once the family's perspective shifts, you must shift the community's perspective as well. I always suggest that once the family agrees on who it is, you should hold focus groups that will enable you to ask key influentials and affluents in the community to help you determine how your family is viewed.

Interestingly, the key imaging/outreach concerns that emerge are consistent for most organizations:

- that the organization's messages are not clear, consistent, and specific;

- that the organization is viewed as a "fair share" charity, not as a priority, for many donors;

- that the organization is perceived as "a player," not as a leader, by the general public and, especially, by major potential donors;

- that many confuse the organization with other similar mission-focused charities;

- that the organization's mission has no urgency, sizzle, or prestige;

- that the organization's purpose is unclear to the community;

- that the organization is seen as impersonal, institutionalized.

Unfortunately, we tend to go to members of our internal family for advice about how well we are doing. To learn the truth about how we are perceived, we must ask uninvolved persons of affluence and influence in our community "how are we doing?"

Focus-group sessions allow you to see how well you are doing in communicating your unique selling proposition to others outside the family.

Goals for the Focus-Group Session

- To provide an opportunity for those of influence in the community to give insights about how your organization is perceived by community leaders

- To encourage suggestions and recommendations for future directions, programs, and services that are consistent with the organization's mission

- To identify interest among those of influence in the community to work with the organization as key volunteers

A focus group is a qualitative research technique. It is a group interviewing method through which attitudes, beliefs, opinions, motivations, and reactions of people can be explored and interchanged with the aid of a trained moderator. A full explanation of focus groups is provided in Appendix B.

Once the organizational vision has been articulated, assigned costs, and refined by the family and representatives of the community you serve, you need to candidly assess if you have a committed group of individuals willing to "give and get" on your organization's behalf. The board is the focus of the next chapter.

CHAPTER FIVE

Developing a Board with Fund-Raising Strengths

> Board members need help in understanding their responsibilities, including "giving and getting," at leadership levels.

Is YOUR NOT-FOR-PROFIT organization in transition? The majority of not-for-profits are formed in response to the specific, often personal, needs of members of the community who take the leadership in creating them. Typically, the initial board members you attract have strong commitments to help the fledgling not-for-profit succeed and grow. Many of the functions board members cheerfully take on are organizational in nature: board members serve as unpaid staff in vital ways, providing professional skills (including accounting, legal advice, and property management) without renumeration.

But, your organization has survived its first years. It now must plan for the next phase. As a not-for-profit positions itself for significant growth, the skills required of its board members will be different: board recruitment should be focused on identifying those with a willingness and ability to provide financial support. *Your board's focus must shift to fund raising.*

> **Not all your current members should continue on in this next phase of board development.**

This transition, though necessary for the organization's survival, can be painful. To sustain your organization's growth requires that the good friends who have shaped the organization's early days take an objective look at their own willingness and ability to provide leadership in "giving and getting." Not all your current members should continue on in this next phase of board development.

In order for board members to willingly undertake their full range of responsibilities, they must understand the commitment they are making to your organization in agreeing to serve.

A job description should be created that provides potential board members with a full explanation of the contract to which they are agreeing. Each board member should be asked at the start of each fiscal year to recommit to that contract.

The board of your organization has three areas of fund-raising responsibilities:

1. Setting and approving development goals and objectives

2. Gift stewardship and accountability

3. Advocacy and asking for money

The board must fully understand what it takes to provide the programs and services your organization's mission commits it to do. Many organizations hesitate to articulate the full package of needs to their boards, fearing the scope will frighten away key volunteers. *This is short-sighted and counterproductive.* If your board has not been involved in creating the "organizational vision" (reread the previous chapter if necessary), it's useful to plan a full-day board retreat with a skilled outside facilitator to help them to appreciate the dimensions of what growth implies.

Gift stewardship and accountability guidelines need to be developed before the development strategy is implemented. Donors are insisting on better accountability and stewardship from not-for-profits. Before an organization can go out and raise money it must establish what gifts are acceptable and how it will handle the gifts it receives. You owe this to potential donors and to your board: *accountability and stewardship are overwhelming concerns for today's—and tomorrow's—donors.*

Review how you will handle specific gift situations which may arise, recover fund-raising costs, and provide donor recognition to others, often serving as volunteers and board members. Once you have formulated the initial answers to these questions, you should create a document titled "Gift Stewardship Guidelines and Policies" which will be available to all concerned. You should also consider adding a line to all fund-raising brochures and reply vehicles indicating that you have a written policy for gift stewardship. Offer to provide a copy upon request. Sample guidelines are given in Appendix A.

Without the board's 100% financial participation, it is difficult to convince members of the broader community to join in the effort.

At the start of each fiscal year board members must be helped to make a "meaningful personal commitment." Obviously, the dollar amount will vary from one person to another; however, board members must make gifts that indicate true commitment.

- **The board's own giving should kick off each fiscal year's fund raising:** All board members should pledge/make their gifts prior to any solicitations taking place in the general community. The board must be approached in a focused, coordinated way if they are to make (and complete) their pledges in a timely manner. The board campaign should begin two months before the start of each new fiscal year with a goal of having pledges and gifts in place by the end of the first month of the new fiscal year.

- **The board must ask.** The executive director furnishing the vision; the board supplying the credibility; and the development director handling the logistics must work together to identify, cultivate, and solicit the individuals, corporations, and foundations from which private support is sought.

Once again, every board member is expected to play an active role in fund raising through both their own financial support, opening doors to others, and general advocacy.

> **Leadership volunteers must be recruited whose primary responsibility will be to ask for money.**

Sometimes the current board won't ask for the truly significant gifts. What can you do? The answer may be to form a leadership group—a foundation, council, or committee—that will.

Only accept as members those who willingly undertake the full range of responsibilities of membership in the leadership group. Make sure prospective members understand the commitment they are making to your organization in agreeing to serve.

A job description should be created that provides potential members with a full explanation of the contract they are entering into. Each member should be asked at the start of each fiscal year to recommit to that contract.

Below is an example of a job description developed for the American Quarter Horse Foundation's Development Council.

The Responsibilities of Members of the Development Council

Purpose:

To enable the American Quarter Horse Foundation to seek financial resources through private support dollars that enable the American Quarter Horse Association to fulfill its mission of education, community outreach, and equine research.

Education	Community Outreach	Research
AJQHA scholarships	Heritage Center/ Museum	Equine research
Racing scholarships	Hall of Fame	
Educational programs	Traveling exhibits	

Nature and Scope:

The American Quarter Horse Foundation has initiated a major expansion of its development and fund-raising activities in conjunction with its upcoming twenty-fifth anniversary in the year 2000.

	Operating	**Capital**	**Endowment**
Community Outreach	Heritage Center $900,000 (yearly)	Hall of Fame $75,000 (one-time)	$10 million*
		Special exhibits $50,000 (yearly)	
		Traveling exhibits $50,000 (yearly)	
		Educational programs $50,000 (yearly)	
Equine Research	$300,000		$5 million
Education	Scholarships $300,000 (yearly)	Educational programs $50,000 (yearly)	$5 million*

TOTALS NEEDED	**$1,500,000 annually**	**$200,000 annually**	**$20,000,000 by 2000**

* $3.2 million already exists in endowment: $2.2 million for the Heritage Center and $1 million for scholarships.

****

Principal Duties and Responsibilities
of Development Council Members

1. Commitment to the goals, objectives, and services of the American Quarter Horse Foundation:

    - Attends board planning retreats and orientation sessions

    - Regular attendance at development council quarterly meetings

    - Participates in major benefit functions and special events

    - Makes a leadership pledge towards the twenty-fifth anniversary campaign

    Development council members are asked to consider a personal contribution of $25,000, payable as $5,000 annually over five years.

2. Willingness and ability to act as spokesperson for the organization:

    - Articulates the goals and objectives to those capable of financially supporting it

    - Promotes the organization to personal, business, media, and other public and/or private contacts

    - Assists in identifying persons and entities capable of financially supporting the organization

    - Expresses appreciation to those who support the American Quarter Horse Foundation through visits, personal notes, and phone calls

3. Willingness and ability to assist in securing of adequate finances for the organization by insuring personal, firm, corporate, service club, or friends' support. Each council member has the responsibility to give or secure a minimum of $25,000 annually each year by:

    - Assisting in the cultivation of key prospects

    - Accompanying others on solicitation visits

****

- **The members of the development council (as well as the board as a whole) must receive regular training to become comfortable with raising money.**

   Most volunteers (and many staff) perceive fund raising as adversarial in nature. Unless they are helped to understand their role as advocates and facilitators, they are understandably reluctant to participate.

   - Plan on holding fund-raising training sessions on a regular basis.

   - Put aside money in your budget to cover the costs of using an experienced facilitator. Remember: you are never a prophet in your own backyard!

And, finally, it is important for your development council and\or board to be representative of the geographic, ethnic, racial, and generational populations it serves and will serve in the near future. Affluence is found in *all* segments of our community. By being inclusive rather than exclusive, your organization will position itself as being relevant to individuals and businesses that may have previously not seen a rationale for supporting your organization.

Next we need to look at the organization: is there an organizational commitment to development? Turning to chapter six, we'll examine the roles of the executive director and the development staff and look at a "must" for competent fund raising: computerization.

CHAPTER SIX

An Organizational Commitment
to Development

> It is *not* logical for the executive director
> to take on the day-to-day
> responsibilities for fund raising.

YOUR ORGANIZATION NEEDS to provide its development department with the resources to implement a successful development program.

The executive director provides the vision; the members of the board furnish the endorsement; the development director handles the logistics that keep the various fund-raising programs moving smoothly along.

While the board provides the community's "seal of approval" and the director of development is responsible for carrying out the logistics of the development program and fund-raising methodologies, it is the role of the executive director to articulate the vision, both internally and externally. For purposes of fund raising, each organization needs to free up its executive director to spend 30 to 50% of his or her time in articulating the vision to potential donors.

The executive director's fund-raising responsibilities include:

- **Serving as the "voice" and the "face" of the organization to donors and prospects.**

The executive director actively cultivates and solicits a small group of key major gift prospects in conjunction with board members and/or the development director.

The executive director should put aside at least one block of time monthly (best blocked out on a regular basis; e.g., last Friday afternoon of each month) for the development director to schedule meetings. The development director should develop a list of prospective donors to be invited to visit with the executive director, either at the organization (if it lends itself to this) or a convenient location. While individual appointments are best, you can host up to three persons together.

The executive director should put aside the necessary time to make a phone call of appreciation to each donor making a gift of over $100—*within 48 hours of receipt of the gift*. The purpose of the call is not to ask for more money but to demonstrate to the donor that your organization considers her or him important.

- thank donor

- ask why he or she supports your organization

- add to the donor's information if appropriate

- offer to visit or send information

- thank again

This call is part of the aftermarketing strategy discussed fully in Part Three.

- **Actively networking within the greater community on a regular basis.**

The development director should work with the executive director to identify all available civic and community organizations such as Rotary, Lions, Chamber, etc., and mutually decide on which ones should be attended regularly and which ones from time to time. Choose at least one organization that the executive director can make a commitment to and volunteer for. Be sure to include some organizations which will bring your executive director into contact with black, Hispanic, and Asian American constituencies.

- **Providing development office with necessary backup and support.**

The executive director is responsible for making sure lines of reporting and accountability are clear to both staff and volunteers.

Each year, he or she should attend one fund-raising conference with the development director for mutual training.

The executive director should support appropriate growth in the development budget and staffing. He or she should also integrate development into management, program, and board functions and help to keep lines of communication open between them.

To fully handle the details that promote a strong development program requires experienced, full-time fund-raising expertise. For the development program to keep pace with the goals and objectives of the organization, the development director must take day-to-day responsibility for the various fund-raising methodologies. He or she handles the many logistics involved in a strong development program including grant writing, major and planned giving, direct mail, phone contact, and special events.

Fund raising takes time and effort: if the organization does not commit to dedicating at least one position to fund raising, it will simply raise less money. Often, the scope of the development program is best served by having both an executive development director and an associate development director. Suggested job descriptions for each position follow.

Director of Development

Reports to: The executive director of development is appointed by and reports to the executive director of the organization.

Nature and Scope: Responsible for the overall development effort including planning, interpretation, coordination, implementation, and management of all fund-raising activities. Advises and makes recommendations to the executive director regarding overall department and organizational goals, objectives, programs, procedures, and policies, wherever fund raising and other appropriate activities are involved.

DUTIES AND RESPONSIBILITIES:

Management of the functions of the development office
- Directs and supervises advancement staff and volunteers
- Serves as staff liaison to the development council
- Oversees the maintenance of the database
- Oversees gift acknowledgment and donor recognition
- Oversees gift stewardship/accountability procedures
- Oversees the development office budget

Develops and implements the organization's development program with emphasis on the following areas of activity
- Major donor cultivation and solicitation
- Planned giving
- Annual giving
- Corporate and foundation grant writing
- Special events

Handles the staffing requirements for major donor and planned giving
- Spends 25-50% of his or her time in face-to-face cultivation of major- and planned-giving donors

REQUIREMENTS:
- Proven success in fund raising in a leadership capacity
- Ability to effectively communicate the mission, goals, and strengths of the organization
- Strong motivational and management skills
- Appropriate education, training, and experience

Associate Development Director

Reports to: The associate development director is appointed by the executive director of the organization at the recommendation of the director of development. She or he reports to the director of development.

Nature and Scope: Responsible for performing specific fund-raising tasks and duties as directed by the director of development, and in accordance with prescribed policies and procedures.

DUTIES AND RESPONSIBILITIES:

Implements the following areas of fund-raising activity
- Annual giving ($250 and under)
- Gift acknowledgment and donor recognition
    * Honor society members
    * Acknowledgement letters
    * Honor roll of donors

Assists with the following areas of fund-raising activity
- Prospect research for major and planned giving
- Corporate and foundation grant writing
- Special events
- Maintenance of the database

REQUIREMENTS:
- Some experience in fund raising in a responsible capacity
- Effective writing and oral communication skills
- Positive interpersonal relationship and team skills
- Appropriate education, training, and experience

The heart of a strong development program lies in its ability to identify, track, and respond personally to its prospects. **Your organization needs to immediately put in place "user-friendly" development software.** Every fund raiser needs to become a "computer wizard." According to Eugene Schwartz, a respected direct-mail author and consultant, "Unless you know how to use your own computer without relying on someone else, you're helpless—and will ultimately be left behind."

Use your database information effectively. The strongest tool you have is your database. But, if you are not coding information about

---

There are two kinds of information available to you for your database:

Internal Information: What your donor gives you

- Number of gifts

- Dates and times

- Amounts

- Causes and reasons

- Addresses and phone numbers

- Personal information (only if you ask)
    - * Supporter preferences for contact (i.e., mail only at Christmas)
    - * Detailed demographics such as age, education, income, and profession

External Information: What you can learn by matching internal donor information to secondary sources

- Census data

- Demographic and lifestyle data

- Specialized database information on media and financial habits

SOURCE: John Rodd & Associates, United Kingdom

donors on it (so as to capture relationships and interests along with transaction histories), you're throwing away powerful clues to your prospects' likely donation triggers. According to the Gartner Group, 98% of all data stored is never analyzed. Take advantage of your database to reveal the wealth of information on your donors.

The creative use of your database is the key to building relationships. According to Ken Burnett, author of *Relationship Fundraising*, to keep proper records of your donors you need to do six things:

1. Choose an adequate system with multiple fields of information.

2. Input data carefully.

3. Undertake continual, thorough cleaning.

4. Update your records continuously with all donor transactions.

5. Regularly add any new information gleaned from correspondence, mailing returns, research, telephone contact, or other sources.

6. Use your data conscientiously and responsibly.

Often, not-for-profits do not have a development system, but rather have a contributions tracking system. Which do you have? You have a contributions tracking system if

- you cannot look at affiliations at a glance;

- it is hard to do queries/sorts;

- the system doesn't "prompt" for flagging or have a usable comments field;

- you must manually enter every salutation;

- the organization of information is not good.

Build a database by answering, **"What data will be needed in order to carry on a meaningful dialogue with donors by mail, by phone, or in person?"**

At a minimum you'll need:

- Name of individual and/or organization

- Mailing address including zip code

- Telephone and fax numbers

- Source of first gift/inquiry along with date and details

- Recency/frequency/monetary purchase history (by date, dollar amounts, area of interest)

- Gift history and rating (scoring)

- Relevant demographic data (age, gender, marital status, family data, education, income, and occupation)

It is strongly recommended that you send for demonstration programs of several development software packages to see the difference between yours and what is available for a modest fee (often as low as $1,800). Each year, *The Chronicle of Philanthropy* and *Fund Raising Management* as well as other publications run special software sections. Get the issues (or back issues) and contact the vendors. Many have free demo disks available.

You should look for the following characteristics in evaluating and choosing fund-development software:

- Does it have a proven track record among not-for-profits?

- It is user-friendly?

- It is fast?

- It is reasonably priced?

- It is flexible in its coding classifications?

- Does the vendor provide ongoing support, via phone, at a reasonable cost?

- Are enhancements provided free, or at a modest cost?

Whatever the software chosen, the development director and support staff must be fully trained and able to use it for gift acknowledging, imputing of data, and standard reports. A terminal must be located in the development director's office, making access to information immediate and ongoing.

In addition to being able to store demographic information, you'll want to be able to segment your donors by gift histories: marked by date of last gift, frequency of giving, monetary value of gifts over life, and last gift amount.

You'll want to be able to segment them by how "close" to your organization they are. Among your *current donors*, are they

- Advocate donors: repeat donors who actively promote your organization to others, often serving as volunteers and board members?

- Client donors: repeat donors who demonstrate loyalty to your organization by consistently "purchasing" a variety of charitable packages (from memorial giving to attending special events as well as a gift to a crisis appeal)?

- Repeat donors: a donor who has made gifts in two consecutive fiscal years?

- Trial donors: making their first gift to your organization?

- Returning donors: making a second gift after a hiatus of a year or more?

In addition, you have

- Lapsed donors: non-responsive for two or more years;

- Prospects: non-donors with a rational reason for being on your database;

- Suspects: non-donors you don't know but think could become prospects.

A regular series of development reports needs to be prepared to enable the development director, executive director and board to track progress toward your goal.

Stick with the basics. Don't get bogged down in a sea of paper. Here are the reports I find most useful:

a. Monthly Contributions Report—listing donors, amounts received, and providing a "rolling total" of progress to date.

b. Campaign Reports—regularly-scheduled analysis by type of fund-raising methodology.

c. Solicitors' Report—regularly-scheduled analysis by volunteer/staff indicating prospect activity.

d. New Prospect Report—for volunteer/staff input on potential contributors, a monthly list of new additions to the database should be prepared.

I also produce a weekly list of donors who have made gifts of over $100. This report goes to the executive director for his or her appreciation phone calls.

Once you have the "basics" of vision, board, and development support in place, you're ready to address the question of finding and keeping your base of support. That's the focus of Part Three.

PART THREE

Creating and Keeping a Base of Support

> There must be a logical base of prospects who are financially capable of supporting the organization's goals and objectives.

To grow from good to great, prioritize your donors and prospects. Match the best prospects with the best strategies. Put the greatest time and effort into working with those who can give the most *and* are most likely to give.

Every not-for-profit faces three fund-raising challenges:

1. Keeping current donors happy so they give more

2. Reconnecting lapsed donors so they give again

3. Persuading new donors to consider giving

There are only two paths for raising funds: acquisition of new donors or renewing existing contributors. Constantly acquiring new donors is the most expensive way to do your fund raising. Many organizations lose money, initially, on every new donor.

According to an NPT/Barna phone survey, almost one-third of the public gives no money to charity outside the church in any given year. And almost half of those who donate to not-for-profits gave to no new organizations last year. While there is a small group of truly philanthropic individuals who donate to a wide variety of charities, the average person, in fact, gave to just 2.6 not-for-profits last year and to only 1.4 organizations they hadn't given to previously. The survey also found that almost half of average active donors (those who donated to a charity in the past 30 days) gave to no new charities last year. While an average active donor gives to 4.6 charities a year, only 1.9 organizations are likely to get a donation if they hadn't received one before.

For most not-for-profits, focusing on renewal and upgrading makes the most sense:

- the demographics of our population support it (increasing longevity and smaller cohorts of young adults)

- the psychographics of current donors support it (mature individuals with "civic" leanings and loyalty)

- the principle of "working smarter, not harder" support it (it takes five times as much work to attract a new donor than to renew an existing one)

This does not mean we ignore acquisition. Rather, we put it in the proper perspective: last, not first. Igor Ansoff's matrix provides a good overview to how we can accomplish increases from both the renewal and acquisition paths:

Directional Policy Matrix (Ansoff)

	Existing Offerings	New Offerings
Existing Markets	PENETRATION (Increase uptake of existing products by existing donors)	PRODUCT DEVELOPMENT (Develop new products for existing donors)
New Markets	MARKET DEVELOPMENT (Find new donors for existing products)	DIVERSIFICATION (New products for new donors)

SOURCE: "The Importance of Strategic Planning," Simon George, *Professional Fund Raising*, October 1994 (UK)

Approximately 70% of your fund-raising efforts should be positioned at cultivating, renewing, and upgrading current and past donors. Your goal is to create "loyal" donors—contributors from whom you can access a larger and larger share of their philanthropic pie.

We must always focus first on the donors we have rather than the prospects we're pursuing.

In chapter seven, we'll explore the value of a renewing donor. "Aftermarketing" (making customers feel good about their purchasing and bringing them back to do more business) is one of today's hottest buzzwords.

In chapters eight and nine, we'll focus on moving first-time and annual donors up the giving pyramid. In chapter eight we'll discuss donor penetration through frequency and upgrading, while chapter nine focuses on donor product expansion through planned giving.

Chapter 10 provides information on the best fund-raising methodology for reaching large groups of lapsed donors: the telephone.

Thirty percent of your fund-raising efforts should be positioned at cultivating and soliciting prospects capable of making more significant gifts. No matter how good a job we do at renewal and upgrading, we must continue to do some selective acquisition.

But we have choices: fund raising doesn't need be done democratically. You can choose who you want to acquire. Finding the best "emergent" markets is the priority. Chapter 11 presents a rationale for focusing on the acquisition of affluent donors rather than the wealthy.

Being selective means choosing prospects with the demographics and psychographics that best work for your organization and its fund-raising "culture." Chapter 12 provides information on some of the population segments you might want to consider making your priority.

CHAPTER SEVEN

The Move to Aftermarketing: Understanding the Value of a Renewing Donor

> **It takes five times as much work to acquire a donor than to renew one.**

THE CHANGING DEMOGRAPHIC paradigm makes the move to renewal and upgrading logical. Satisfied donors are repeat donors. *If you lose a donor, you must find a new one.* It makes more sense to focus on keeping and increasing the support from those who already give.

What happens if you focus on increasing and renewals? Answer: You grow from good to great!

According to Mal Warwick, "After 10 years of haphazard solicitation, (only) 10 out of 100 donors remain. With 10% improvement on results each year, more than 30 remain."

Let's put that another way: *Renew, renew, renew.* A 5% rise in customer loyalty increases profits by 60% or greater!

By focusing on increasing your organization's donor renewal rate by 10% or better in each succeeding year—with an ultimate goal of achieving as close to 100% as possible—you will be able to position for gains of 25% and greater each year. An advantage of focusing on renewal is that it reduces your reliance on acquisition.

> **For many organizations, growing is "pushing a boulder uphill" because you first have to replace significant numbers of lost donors.**

What is your organization's annual renewal rate? Figure this out immediately! If, for example, you currently have a renewal rate of 60%, typical for many not-for-profits, *you are automatically losing 40% of your donors in the second year.*

By setting goals of moving from the current 60% renewal rate, increasing first to 70%, then to 80%, and reaching 90% in year three, your organization will be able to concentrate on moving ahead rather than replacing large numbers of donors.

Below is an example of an organization that started with 3,000 donors making an average gift of $32 in year one.

Dollars Raised from Renewing Donors

Year 1: 3000 donors @ $32	Year 2: 60% 1,800 donors	Year 2: 75% 2,250 donors	Year 2: 90% 2,700 donors
$96,000 raised	$57,600 raised	$72,000 raised	$86,400 raised

Notice the vast difference as to where the organization winds up, depending on its renewal rate. In year two:

- with a 60% renewal rate, it loses 1,200 donors;

- with a 75% renewal rate, it loses 750 donors;

- with a 90% renewal rate, it loses 300 donors.

Remember: before you can grow, you need to replace the donors you lost.

What does focusing on renewal rather than acquisition really mean for your organization?

- You don't have to work as hard to replace large numbers of donors, incurring expensive acquisition costs.

- You have the opportunity to focus, instead, on upgrading the current donors.

> **Aim for a 96% renewal rate.**

Most not-for-profits settle for an annual donor renewal rate well below the 96% optimum rate. My research shows that annual renewal rates of 40, 50, and 60% are common. No wonder it's so hard to grow significantly!

Creating an Aftermarketing Program

The key to successful fund raising is to keep the donors you have. To do that requires structuring a development program that focuses on what occurs *after* the gift is made. Ken Burnett calls this "relationship fund raising"; Terry Varvas calls this "aftermarketing."

Regardless of how you label it, the recipe for successful aftermarketing includes some basic ingredients like respect, open communication, and trust.

Harold Brierley, a pioneer in the development of Relationship Management™, categorizes the fundamentals of relationship management into six major areas:

1. Building the framework

2. Establishing the relationship

3. Developing an ongoing dialogue

4. Maximizing the value of the relationship

5. Rewarding loyalty

6. Sustaining the relationship

Building the Framework

Customer service is either good or not. The customer's perception of the situation *is* reality. *Twenty-six of every 27 customers who have a bad experience won't complain.* But, 90% of them won't come back either.

You can gain an average of 6% a year in market share simply by providing good service—satisfying and keeping your donors:

- Only 4% of unhappy donors bother to complain.

- For every complaint you hear, most organizations have about 26 customers with problems, 6 of which are serious.

- The average customer who has had a problem with an organization tells 9 to 10 people about it. Thirteen percent retell the experience to more than 20 people.

- A customer with a positive experience will tell 3 to 5 people. Therefore, it takes 3 to 4 happy customer experiences to make up for one negative one.

SOURCE: *Building Customer Loyalty*, Barbara A. Glanz, Irwin, 1994

Robert Bly, writing in *Keeping Clients Satisfied*, cautions that "service must be consistently good. One small lapse can undo, in a moment, a relationship that took weeks, months, or years to achieve.

"First-time buyers are testing you without a large risk or investment. If they like what they get, they'll probably come back for more. If they don't, they figure they haven't lost much."

Once you decide that a major development goal is to "keep and enhance donor relationships," you begin to look at your acknowledgment, appreciation, and recognition vehicles in a new light. Rather than viewing these as necessary but somewhat irritating tasks, to be completed as quickly as possible so you are freed up to move on to another donor, *acknowledgment, appreciation and recognition become the backbone of your cultivation efforts.*

> **Nordstrom department store has the following customer service motto: "Respond to unreasonable customer requests."** The store notes they've never been unable to oblige. *Once relationship marketing is your positioning, everything becomes possible.*

How does your perspective change in relationship marketing? Some examples:

- **The office is set up to serve the donor.**

Donor needs take priority. Questions and concerns are responded to within minutes, not hours or days. All front-line personnel are chosen and trained for their people skills. They are encouraged to use their initiative and to prevent donors from being shuffled from one department to another.

Donor requests are met without protest regardless of the effort it takes to accomplish them. Donors are *never* made to feel their requests are inconvenient or unreasonable. Changes in addresses, corrections to records are done cheerfully.

- **Each employee and volunteer understands she or he is responsible for her or his own behavior towards the donor.**

When employees and volunteers are pleasant, cooperative, and resourceful in taking care of the customer, the donor tends to generalize this experience to your overall image.

You need to encourage your employees and volunteers to be friendly, flexible, and focused on immediate problem solving and speedy recovery.

- **Focus on creating a group of "core" donors.**

"Core" donors are the ultra-loyal contributors who make multiple gifts within a 12-month period and who serve as your endorsers to other, less committed individuals.

Establish a strong aftermarketing matrix—a series of recultivation steps that begins with the acknowledgment of the latest gift. (This is described in detail in the next chapter.)

Look for as many ways to indicate your appreciation as possible. Provide as many "value-added" services as you can.

When Should You Show Appreciation?

Eight times to do "Value Addeds":

- For the good, solid, steady, no-complaints, no-noise donor.
- For the donor who has done you the favor of complaining.
- For the new donor who has just made a second donation.
- For a donor who has thanked you.
- For a donor who's had a tough time.
- When going out of your way will prevent a donor from having a problem.
- For a good donor who has the potential for bringing you new donors or increasing his/her giving.
- To make employees and volunteers feel good about serving.

SOURCE: *Managing Knock Your Socks Off Service*, Chip Bell and Ron Zemke.

Establishing the Relationship

Rethink your relationship with donors. G.T. "Buck" Smith, former president of Chapman College, notes that "We are in a business of dollars and cents. So we tend to think of donors not as people, but rather, as financial opportunities."

As a result, once a gift is made, many development officers feel the "solicitation cycle" is complete. Your donor, on the other hand, believes your relationship is *just beginning*!

Terry Varva, writing in *Aftermarketing: How to Keep Customers For Life Through Relationship Marketing*, reminds us that "from the customer's perspective, a purchase is most likely viewed as *initiating* a relationship. The customer feels considerable desire or need for a continued interaction with the selling organization."

Sam Walton, founder of WalMart, America's most successful retail chain, understood the importance of customer loyalty. Walton asserted, "That's where the real profit lies, not in trying to drag strangers into your store for a one-time purchase based on splashy sales or expensive advertising."

Developing an Ongoing Dialogue

"Good" is not good enough. Of those who respond to customer-satisfaction surveys, 95% of those indicating "excellent" will purchase again or recommend to friends; but at the "good" level, only 60% will purchase again.

Don't ignore the two basic factors in building donor loyalty:

1. Donor satisfaction with the way you respond to their gifts; and

2. Donor satisfaction with your organization.

Sad to say, we rarely take these factors into consideration. In fact, market research has shown that the largest share of donor attrition is actually a cost of doing business poorly. In other words:

Of every 100 individuals who stop supporting you, just 4 are "irretrievable" because they move away or die:

- Fifteen have made a decision that another organization can serve them better.

- Fifteen are unhappy with your organization.

- Sixty-six think you don't care about them.

• **Fifteen have made a decision that another organization can serve them better.** Usually, the decision not to renew is made by default. In other words, because your organization has not provided the donor with enough information for her or him to see the not-for-profit as "unique," Ms. or Mr. Jones assumes that another organization can just as easily solve the problem or meet her or his needs.

Donors crave information and education. Because of the increasingly sophisticated delivery of information, your donors expect you to provide more and better explanations of what you do and how you do it. Donors have access to more information than ever before and, because individuals are more skeptical of claims and promises, they tend to study appeals more carefully. And, increasingly, the donor is proactive in seeking out the information s/he desires. Be prepared to elicit feedback from donors and adjust your strategies to meet their needs and suggestions. Educated donors will make your organization more competitive.

Your not-for-profit should devise a "positioning statement." Use this consistently in all literature to remind donors and prospects of who you are and what you do.

Here, once again, is the positioning statement used by the Columbia River Girl Scout Council. In one form or another, it appears on all Council literature:

> The Columbia River Girl Scout Council supports 18,667 girls, young women, and adults in 4 Neighborhood Service Teams and 1,056 troops in 13 counties in Southwest Washington and Northwest Oregon along the Columbia River, covering 33,500 square miles. One girl in nine in our community belongs to Girl Scouting. We help these valuable young women to meet the growing responsibilities of our families, social institutions, communities, nation, and world through innovative programs which are educational and preventative in nature—and fun!

The Columbia River Girl Scout Council uses a consistency of design elements to educate as well:

- a photo of happy girls from diverse backgrounds appears on each communications piece, reply vehicle, and outer envelope

- common phrases such as "Join us in shaping their future" and, "It costs $110.04 to support one girl in Girl Scouts for a year" are used on each appeal

- "Girl Scout" green is the accent color on all fund-raising appeals

• **Fifteen are unhappy with your organization.** While a satisfied customer will send 5 people your way, a disgruntled customer can be counted on to bad-mouth you to 15 to 20 of his or her acquaintances.

Up to 95% of unhappy donors won't complain directly. Instead, they'll tell others, negatively, about you: most will tell 10 to 12 people, but a vocal minority, about 13%, will tell 20 or more others about their unhappy experiences. *The bottom line: it takes 12 positive incidents to make up for 1 negative incident.*

We view a customer who is complaining as a real blessing in disguise. He or she is someone we can resell.

—Louis Carbone, VP, National Car Rental

Look at complaining donors as your friends. They are signaling your organization that trouble lies ahead. Michael LeBoeuf, writing in *How to Win Customers and Keep Them for Life*, suggests that you:

- seek out and welcome complaints;
- take every complaint seriously;
- get people at the top actively involved in listening to and resolving complaints;
- document and classify complaints;
- set goals for resolving complaints;
- learn and improve from complaints.

Even worse, when donors do complain we often increase their unhappiness. You have to deal with both the donor's feelings and with solving the problem. If you solve the problem without addressing the anger, your donor probably won't renew:

- Keep your cool
- Listen with empathy and for the facts
- Take action to solve the donor's problem
- Bring the incident to a polite close
- Don't expect to win them all

Remember, 95% of those who complain will donate again if their complaint is resolved quickly and with caring.

Your current donors are your most powerful advertisement. The better you satisfy them, the more likely they are to tell others about your organization. Word-of-mouth endorsements are often the most influential source of information. More Americans rely on advice and information from friends and family than turn to the media as a "best source."

But, few donors will tell anyone about good experiences unless you ask them to. Put in place an automatic program to request endorsements and testimonials. How? Ask them!

Here's a tip: A P.S. (with an enclosed reply card) at the bottom of an acknowledgment letter will encourage those donors with the strongest feelings to communicate back to you. Gather these endorsements and run them in your newsletter as an article or use them on your appeals, reply envelopes, annual reports, etc.

• **Sixty-six out of every 100 people who stop supporting you think you don't care about them.** According to 32% of those polled, the biggest customer service mistake is failing to make the customer feel important. Only 6% of customers think the service they receive from organizations is excellent. Forty-five percent say it is good, while 43 percent say fair, and 5% say it is poor.

Maximizing the Value of the Relationship, Rewarding Loyalty, and Sustaining the Relationship

> **"The deepest principle of human nature**
> **is a craving to be appreciated."**
>
> **—William James, father of American psychology**

Recognition is one of the most fundamental motivational needs. Author Richard Lynch, writing in *LEAD!: How Public and*

Nonprofit Managers Can Bring Out the Best in Themselves and Their Organizations, reminds us that:

- those who don't get recognition positively often get it through negative behavior (not renewing);
- recognition must be given frequently;
- recognition must be varied;
- recognition must be honest;
- recognition must be appropriate to the act;
- recognition must be consistent;
- recognition must be timely;
- recognition must be individualized as much as possible.

What Do Donors Want?

A study by Carnegie Mellon University revealed that contributors want

- reminders about pledges—preferably a brief reminder notice
- thoughtfulness—don't call during dinner hours
- information—let them know the impact of their gifts (how they were used)
- special appreciation for first-time gifts
- acknowledgments: a phone call without a solicitation
- news about the organization

The health of your organization depends on the loyalty of your donors, and loyal donors are not created by chance. There are four keys to gaining donor allegiance:

1. Acknowledge the donor as a person—an individual with a name, a life, needs, and concerns

2. Learn everything you can about each of your donors

3. Ask what each donor wants from you, and deliver it

4. Make it easy to do business with your organization

1. Acknowledge the donor as a person—an individual with a name, a life, needs, and concerns. Because it is more efficient to renew and upgrade donors than to continuously seek out new prospects, donor recognition is a key to a strong development program. In addition, a donor recognition program helps to educate and encourage new contributors to place their support at a higher level.

Thank them properly.

- Make a phone call and/or send out your acknowledgment letters within 48 hours.

- Acknowledge *all* donors regardless of the size of their gifts.

- Show your donors you know who they are by indicating if they are new donors, ongoing supporters, renewing after an absence, etc. Segment your donors by gift histories: marked by recency of last gift, frequency of giving, monetary value of gifts over life, and last gift amount.

- Keep your mailing lists clean. Make sure salutations are correct and addresses current.

Let your donors know you're thinking about them. Acknowledge them constantly. Thank them in your honor roll, send congratulatory cards for birthdays, promotions, graduations (anything you can congratulate them for), send holiday greetings, provide a special newsletter of their own, a "VIP" phone contact, etc.

Know their interests. Keep a list of their professional and personal interests. If you see an article that is pertinent, clip it and send it off with a brief, handwritten note. Most donors only hear from charities asking for money.

Reward loyalty. At least 80% of your donations come from 20% of your base.

- Create a tiered recognition program for $100 and above donors. A formal donor-recognition program helps to educate and encourage contributors to place their support at a higher level.

- Create exclusive benefits and services. Increase opportunities for even more personal involvement and interaction with your organization.

- Give these "core" donors a sense of belonging to the "family."

- Encourage other donors to aspire to that special donor level.

- Establish an opportunity cost for failure to stay loyal. For example, a missing tab on a plaque for the year of non-participation.

- Provide unanticipated rewards to build and sustain loyalty.

2. Learn everything you can about each of your donors. If you don't ask your donors for information, you won't get it. You need to put in place vehicles that consistently ask for information in a format you can record on your database.

Develop a customer profile. Get a clear picture of both the donor you have *and* the prospect you want to attract. What's their age range, income level, gender, marital status, educational level, occupation, and lifestyle? What matters to them? The more you can zero in on who you are targeting as supporters, the easier it will be to communicate about your organization through their eyes.

Create a donor survey. This is the single best vehicle for collecting usable demographic and psychographic information. Send it as part of the welcoming packet to all donors. Be sure you explain:

- the benefit to the respondent;

- the objective of the survey;

- how the respondent was selected;

- the importance of the survey;

- the confidentiality and privacy involved;
- where to send the result;
- when you want it back.

An example of a donor survey is found in chapter 13.

3. Ask what each donor wants from you and deliver it. Involve your donors.

- Host low-key, no-pressure get-togethers to increase donor awareness of your programs and services and to build relationships.

- Ask them why they support you. Use their testimonials in your annual report, appeals, and newsletters.

- Solicit their recommendations for improving your service delivery. Give them credit when you act on their ideas.

- Conduct written and telephone surveys on a regular basis. Ask donors for advice and deliver on their suggestions.

- Hold focus-group meetings on a regular basis. A focus group is a process for gathering information rather than a forum for developing solutions. (A full explanation of how to conduct a focus group is found in Appendix B.)

- Let the donor shape the project, going beyond donor involvement to donor leadership.

- Get all your staff and volunteers, often in groups, to visit donors. Visit donors again and again.

Respect donors. Remember Nordstrom's motto: "Respond to unreasonable customer requests." This philosophy leads employees to relish the challenges that customers toss at them.

- Always return phone calls. If you can't personally make the call, delegate the task—but make contact.

- Keep your word. If something goes wrong, inform your donors and prospects immediately and keep them informed until the situation is rectified to their satisfaction.

- Be professional. Check all printed materials for accuracy. Mistakes cause donors to worry about your accountability.

- Donors have rights. Follow the credo developed by the National Society of Fund Raising Executives, et al., included below.

4. Make it easy to do business with your organization. Create a new-donor welcome program. Put some effort into identifying what your new donor will appreciate receiving: in addition to the thank-you letter, you might include a "hotline" phone number for any questions, a short fact sheet that summarizes your organization, and a case example of what gifts accomplish.

There's no shortage of specific ideas we can use to keep our donors involved and caring. *The dilemma lies in organizing the multitude of aftermarketing concepts in a framework that your organization uses consistently to create "apostles"—donors with core loyalty.* Chapter eight focuses on how to achieve this greater donor penetration.

A Donor Bill of Rights

PHILANTHROPY is based on voluntary action for the common good. It is a tradition of giving and sharing that is primary to the quality of life. To assure that philanthropy merits the respect and trust of the general public, and that donors and prospective donors can have full confidence in the not-for-profit organizations and causes they are asked to support, we declare that all donors have these rights:

ARTICLE ONE: To be informed of the organization's mission, of the way the organization intends to use donated resources, and of its capacity to use donations effectively for their intended purposes.

ARTICLE TWO: To be informed of the identity of those serving on the organization's governing board, and to expect the board to exercise prudent judgment in its stewardship responsibilities.

ARTICLE THREE: To have access to the organization's most recent financial statements.

ARTICLE FOUR: To be assured their gifts will be used for the purposes for which they were given.

ARTICLE FIVE: To receive appropriate acknowledgment and recognition.

ARTICLE SIX: To be assured that information about their donations is handled with respect and with confidentiality to the extent provided by law.

ARTICLE SEVEN: To expect all relationships with individuals representing organizations of interest to the donor will be professional in nature.

ARTICLE EIGHT: To be informed whether those seeking donations are volunteers, employees of the organization, or hired solicitors.

ARTICLE NINE: To have the opportunity for their names to be deleted from mailing lists that an organization may intend to share.

ARTICLE TEN: To feel free to ask questions when making a donation and to receive prompt, truthful, and forthright answers.

Developed by: AAFRC, AHP, CASE, NSFRE and endorsed by Independent Sector, NCDC, NCPG, NCRD, and United Way of America.

CHAPTER EIGHT

Creating Apostles:
Donor Penetration through
Frequency and Upgrading

> It's better to have 100% of 10% of the market than
> 10% of 100% of it. The numbers of customers are
> the same, but the costs are far different.

YOU'LL RAISE MORE money upgrading renewing donors than chasing after new prospects. It's easier to sell an upgrade than an initial gift. Think about what happens when you go house hunting. The realtor asks your price ceiling. "Oh," you say, "certainly not more than $110,000." What does she take you to see? Houses at $115,000 and $120,000. Why? She knows you've made up your mind to spend the $110,000—she just needs to persuade you to upgrade.

Let's return to our example from the previous chapter. Look what happens if you add modest upgrades of 10 and 20%.

Dollars Raised from Renewing Donors			
Year 1: 3000 donors @ $32	**Year 2: 60% 1,800 donors**	**Year 2: 75% 2,250 donors**	**Year 2: 90% 2,700 donors**
$96,000 raised	$57,600 raised	$72,000 raised	$86,400 raised
10% Upgrade	$63,360 raised	$79,200 raised	$95,040 raised
20% Upgrade	$76,032 raised	$95,400 raised	$103,680 raised

CONCLUSION: If you add a focus of upgrading to your renewal strategy, you can surpass what you raised previously with the smaller pool of donors with less work. It takes five times as much effort to attract a new donor as to renew and upgrade an existing one.

Not everyone cares about your organization. The general public may have some awareness and interest in your organization, but won't necessarily act on that information. Even among the small percentage of total prospects who do form your logical audience, there are differences in interest level:

- **Users**—have an affiliation with your organization, based on making use of its programs and services. They are often unwilling to donate or only willing to make token gifts because they "pay" their way.

- **Vested Individuals**—have some ownership of your organization, which may be tenuous at this time. Often volunteers, sometimes staff, they "give their time" but can be educated to understand their financial commitment.

- **Supporters**—have both involvement with and commitment to your organization. These are the advocates we need.

Using aftermarketing and increased communication, our first goal is to move our audiences along to become supporters. Once that initial goal is achieved, in the interests of working smarter rather than harder, our strategy should be:

- Keeping current donors happy so they give more
  (CREATING SUPPORTERS)

- Reconnecting lapsed donors so they give again
  (RECONNECTING VESTEDS)

- Persuading new donors to consider giving
  (EDUCATING USERS)

Focusing on Users to Create "Core" Donors

Pareto's principle—the 80:20 analysis—reminds us that about 20% of your donors account for 80% of your donations. Put another way, this means that the vast majority of private gifts are attributable to a few donors.

Therefore, **if you have a number of loyal customers who commit to you, who make you their philanthropic priority and support you consistently, your organization should focus on meeting these "core" donors' needs.**

This concept fits well with the idea of lifelong value. When you use the following formula, the value of a seemingly modest donor adds up quickly:

> **Amount of money spent annually $_____**
> **x the length in years of the relationship _____**
> **= the lifetime value of the donor $_____**

But, too often fund raisers don't bother to calculate what a loyal donor is worth to the organization over the years.

At the 14th International Fund Raising Workshop held in the Netherlands, consultant John Rodd discussed the implications of Pareto's Law for fund raisers. His research suggests that *only the top 30% of donors make a profit for our organizations.* We break even with the 40th percentile and *lose money with the 50 to 100th percentile*!

You will find case examples that utilize the principles in this chapter in Part Four.

William A. Sherden, writing in *Market Ownership: The Art & Science of Becoming #1*, concurs:

> "The customer profitability problem is so widespread and acute that the conventional 80/20 rule should be amended to become the 80/20/30 rule: The top 20% of customers generate 80% of the company's profits, half of which is lost serving the bottom 30% of unprofitable customers."

Rodd's findings should sound a warning to us all. We must recognize the impact and importance of the few who move us ahead and we should make efforts to manage them with care.

Specifically, your development program must:

- create high-level donor programs and special ways of recognizing and rewarding donors' contributions to your cause;

- understand that the loss of these golden donors would be catastrophic—so your customer care and service mechanisms should be in place and regularly exercised;

- consider how the "profitability" of this segment allows you to make a case for investing more in them;

- apply donor market research to know them better.

Doing a better job with "core" donors is far less expensive than trying, constantly, through a random approach to acquire the same number of new donors who may—or may not—have much interest in your not-for-profit.

"Your customers are only satisfied because their expectations are so low and because no one else is doing better. Just having satisfied customers isn't good enough anymore. If you really want a booming business, you have to create Raving Fans."

SOURCE: *Raving Fans: A Revolutionary Approach to Customer Service*, Ken Blanchard and Sheldon Bowles, William Morrow & Co., 1993

Remember, it takes five times as much effort to attract a new donor as to renew and upgrade an existing one. *Measure success not in terms of market share, but rather in terms of share of customer.*

There is a spectrum of donor interaction, reflecting the duration and depth of donors' relationship with your organization. Again, deferring to John Rodd, the degree of interaction varies from:

- Trial donor—the first time or experimental donor

- Repeat donor—second, third time. This would-be donor is getting warmer towards you

- Regular donor—the committed supporter

- Loyal/longer-term donor—invested in our cause

- Committed donor—totally on your side, the classic advocate or apostle. In their eyes you can do no wrong

Because a 5% increase in customer loyalty can produce profit increases from 25 to 85%, focus on the quality of market—including the depth of the relationship and the level of customer satisfaction.

Your goal is to create "apostles"—customers so satisfied that they convert the uninitiated to your organization.

Focus on the Earliest Stages of the Relationship

Your donors' view of their relationship with your organization is *front-loaded.* In other words, what happens during the earliest stages of the relationship carries a disproportionate weight in shaping their feelings towards you.

This makes sense; as I mentioned earlier in this book, donors and organizations view "the gift" from different perspectives. The donor sees it as opening the cycle of the relationship while the not-for-profit views it as the culmination of steps of cultivation and solicitation. As a result, your organization often hesitates to continue communication just as the donor feels most receptive to hearing from you!

The first 45 days are crucial. You need to develop a "Welcome Aboard" program—a formalized aftermarketing matrix—that encourages strong bonding during the early phase of your donor relationship.

> **A donor who has just made a gift feels good about her- or himself. This is the best time to approach her or him again with additional information and opportunities for connection more strongly with your organization.**

The "Welcome Aboard" program is a formalized multi-step program that encourages donors who have made a first gift within the fiscal year to consider a second gift as soon as possible. It contains alternative steps for your organization to follow, depending on donor response. Typically it segments (minimally) donors at above and below $100. Depending on your organization's capacity for follow-through and ability to identify additional criteria, you might also consider segmenting by new, renewing, and upgraded donors and by demographic and psychographic similarities and differences.

The objective of the aftermarketing matrix is to respond to the donor's positioning that *the relationship is just beginning* by front-loading cultivation steps and creating a logical climate for a second ask.

> **"Making the donor a partner, exceeding expectations, and delighting customers on the basis of service, design, and originality may be the differentiators and selling points for the future."**
>
> Finding donors is not enough: how business will secure them in the future will grow increasingly critical. As donors feel less and less loyal to organizations and hide themselves behind voice mail or answering machines, it will become increasingly difficult to forge and secure enduring donor relationships.
>
> SOURCE: adapted from *FUTURE TENSE: The Business Realities of the Next Ten Years*, Ian Morrison and Greg Schmid, William Morrow & Co., 1994

Typically, the aftermarketing matrix steps include:

- acknowledging the donor's gift within 48 hours
- demonstrating appreciation of the donor's "specialness"
- soliciting information about and listening to the donor

- providing additional information about the organization

- offering the opportunity to make a second gift

(Chapter 13 provides an aftermarketing matrix example.)

Here are specific things to do for each step:

Acknowledging the donor's gift within 48 hours

Donors want to know, quickly, that you've received their gifts. Within 48 hours you need to provide them with some indication that that has happened. Depending on your organization's ability to respond, this could be accomplished with:

- a personalized letter;

- a card or post card indicating a personalized letter and/or receipt will follow;

- a telephone call.

Demonstrating appreciation of the donor's "specialness"

Your donor wants to know that you know who she or he is. A new donor? A renewing contributor? A committed partner upgrading her or his gift? *Make sure the letter of appreciation you send is personal, not just personalized.*

For example, Northwest Medical Teams International (NMTI) lets new donors know they are special. It doesn't take much for NMTI to demonstrate it knows its donors. Just a line or two:

> "As the chairman of the board of Northwest Medical Teams International, I want to welcome you as a member of "The Team!" Your recent contribution is deeply appreciated and will help continue to bring assistance to those in need around the world . . . We hope you will consider becoming a regular contributor so we can continue to help more and more people."

A tip: Create a special envelope just for your donors. A regular #10 can be customized for your special friends through the addition of the words "Thank you!" in script.

Soliciting information about and listening to the donor

Columbia River Girl Scout Council congratulates $100-and-greater donors on achieving membership in the Juliette Gordon Low Society. Enclosed with their letter of appreciation is a brochure that asks for feedback: how they want to be listed on the honor roll (or not listed at all), and it allows $100-and-greater donors to request a certificate of appreciation.

Perhaps the best action step is the feedback of personal information about the donor. A donor survey can be used, for example, to encourage such feedback. An example of a survey is provided in chapter 13.

While you can combine this step with the acknowledgment, you can also choose to use it as a second cultivation step. Your goal is to encourage the donor to take action in response. In the example of the Columbia River Girl Scouts used in chapter 13, under-$100 donors receive it along with their letter of appreciation. One-hundred-dollar-and-over donors receive the survey in a separate "Welcoming Packet" mailing.

Providing additional information about the organization

In order to make your organization a priority, donors need to decide they want to offer more than token support. That takes information.

Many organizations mistakenly assume that, because the donor has made a gift, he or she knows the unique selling proposition of the not-for-profit. Don't assume! *Continue to educate your donor.*

The U.S. Committee for UNICEF sends, within a week of the acknowledgment letter, a "New Donor" packet. Adopt the practice: if not for all donors, at least to new ones or to those who give over $100.

Your packet—an oversized 9" x 12" envelope with "Thank You" or "Urgent: Donor Information" emblazoned on it—might consist of:

- a donor survey;

- a copy of the most recent newsletter;

- a fact sheet or overview brochure;

- business cards of the director of development and executive director.

Listening to the Voice of the Customer

- Customer surveys
- Customer follow-up
- Customer contact
- Customer councils
- Focus groups
- Interviews
- Electronic mail
- 800-numbers

- Customer-service training
- Test marketing
- Quality guarantees
- Inspectors
- Ombudsmen
- Complaint-tracking system
- Suggestion boxes

Source: *Reinventing Government*, David Osborne and Ted Gaebler, Addison-Wesley, 1992

Offering the opportunity to make a second gift

Let your donors know—sooner, not later—you consider them part of a small group willing to consider making your organization a priority. **Ask them within 30 days to give again,** making sure they understand *why* you've come back to them. The reason? They are special. Only *they* have given to you. Isn't it logical to invite them to give again?

In the case of our aftermarketing matrix example in chapter 13, donors who gave less than $100 as their first gift receive an invitation to consider making a second gift that will bring them to the Leadership Society level. Donors of over $100 receive an invitation to consider making a "partnership gift": a selection of specific examples of gifts ranging from $250 and greater.

Offering Choices in Fulfillment Mechanisms

According to a Gallup survey of American donors, 38% of contributors said they wish they could have given more. Joan Flanagan, author of *Successful Fundraising* and *The Grass Roots Fundraising Book*, notes that "Pledges are the perfect strategy to make this happen."

Wouldn't you feel more satisfied giving a large enough gift to make a difference?

For many people, the problem is not motivation, it's fulfillment. Assume *you'd* like to make a gift of $1,000 or more. How likely are you to write a one-time check for that amount?

Consider, instead, positioning a $1,000 gift as:

- $250 quarterly for one year

or

- $83.33 monthly for one year

or

- $19.23 weekly for one year

Also, offer your donor the option to fulfill his or her gift without the quarterly/monthly/weekly checkwriting: via bank draft or credit card.

Focus on Monthly Giving

Monthly donors contribute 7 to 12 years. That's at least *3 times longer* than an annual giver. Monthly gifts tend to range from $15 to $30, with some as high as $125.

Three to five percent of your donor base will convert to a monthly giving program if asked. Many will upgrade their gifts more than 100% and, because they are among the most loyal of donors, up to 40% will respond as well to a "special appeal."

SOURCE: "How to build a highly profitable monthly donor program," video from Harvey McKinnon, Strathmoor Press

---

A steady stream of donations quickly builds value. Annual donors typically contribute about 2 years before their contributions lapse. During this brief period, donors will give $25 to $100 per year. The cumulative value of the annual donations, $50 to $200, falls in the small, shaded ares in the lower left corner of the following chart.

The shaded area highlights the cumulative value of monthly donations within the $15 to $30 range.

- A $25 donor gives $180 the first year. That's as much as you make in 2 years with an annual donor. Over 7 years, your donor contributes $1,260!

- A $30 donor gives $360 the first year, three times more than an annual donor. By year 7, your donor contributes $2,520 *excluding upgrades or special appeals.*

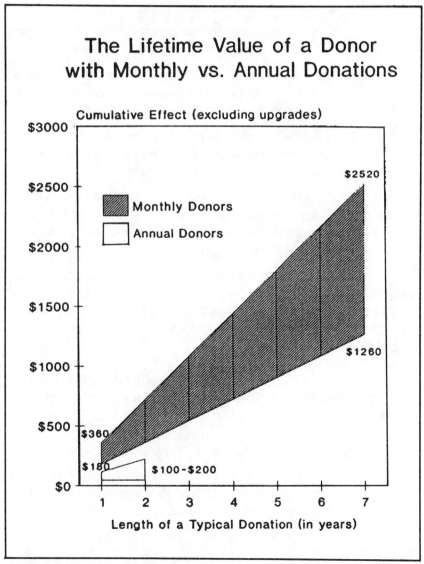

The Lifetime Value of a Donor with Monthly vs. Annual Donations

Cumulative Effect (excluding upgrades)

Monthly Donors

Annual Donors

$2520

$1260

$360

$180

$100-$200

Length of a Typical Donation (in years)

Source: Harvey McKinnon Associates, 1993

In *Targeted Fund Raising: Defining and Refining your Development Strategy*, I noted that "To reach the higher dollar amounts in annual giving, you'll have to encourage use of the fund-raising vehicle that makes giving less painful: pledging." Today's changing paradigms support this concept more than ever.

Frequent giving increases donor loyalty as well as gift levels. Not only will you get more money through pledging, you will be more likely to retain your annual donor. Steve Woodworth, vice president of marketing at World Vision, makes four points about monthly givers:

1. Monthly pledging breaks the psychological barrier. Donors who would not consider themselves $200 donors will make a commitment to send $20 per month.

2. It's the ultimate involvement device. With monthly pledges, "donors consider themselves more a part of the organization and are less likely to lose interest."

3. Gift income from monthly pledges is more stable than income from once-a-year gifts; "it is more predictable and it is less influenced by the general climate."

4. If you're using high-cost acquisition vehicles, monthly pledges are sometimes the only way to acquire new donors and show a profit. A $20 gift "sells" more easily than a $240 gift.

It's also easier to generate an additional gift for emergency appeals or a special cause from monthly donors: up to 40% of your core donors will give an extra gift when asked. And, 80 to 90% of planned gifts and major gifts come from people who have been members or annual donors for 3 to 5 years!

A caution: while the concept of upgrading donations through monthly giving is simple, it requires a firm commitment to managing the program.

Bonnie O'Neill, vice president of Meyer Partners, notes that

- monthly donors need a special communication plan. You can't send a donor who has made a monthly pledge commitment the same direct-mail appeals developed for less-frequent donors. Monthly pledgers don't need to be "sold," just reminded.

- Successful pledge programs rely on accurate gift records. You must develop a pledge-tracking system that signals when a donor falls behind on a pledge commitment. Your reminder to these very special donors must be sensitive.

Case Example:
Monthly Donors Surpass Annual Givers

A prominent public interest group made an appeal to three groups: new members, established members, and others who had recently declined. All were invited to become automatic monthly givers.

The results:

- Twenty-eight percent of those who responded became automatic monthly donors. This compared with 72% who gave a one-time gift.

- Over the next year, those who became automatic monthly donors contributed 69% of the revenue generated by the appeal. Annual givers contributed only 31% of total revenue.

- Monthly donors' gifts averaged $10 per month, or $120 per year. Before enrolling, these donors had contributed $25 to $50 per year.

- The lifetime value of the automatic monthly donors will exceed $275,000.

SOURCE: Clearing House Initiators, NY, NY

Electronic Fund Transfer (EFT), through the Automated Clearing House (ACH), is an idea whose time has arrived.

Back in the early 1980s I tried to interest my donors in making their gifts via bank draft. To my dismay, almost no one was interested. Today I understand that response was logical: my donors were overwhelmingly Depression and World War II Babies, uncomfortable with the new technology.

But increasingly, if not already, the majority of your donors are going to be Boomers and Busters. For them, EFT is a logical choice. *Monthly giving plans (through pledging), standing credit card payments, bank drafts, and electronic fund transfer are the wave of the future.*

Using EFT provides numerous advantages to both the donor and the organization:

For the donor

- Convenience of payment

- No charge for using service

- Donations appear clearly on bank statements

For the organization

- Cash flow is better because you know, in advance, the date you will receive access to funds.

- Because processing costs are less, more of the donation is put to use.

- You eliminate monthly statements and reminders.

Remember your obligations: loyalty goes both ways. Unfortunately for not-for-profits, we continue to "just not get it."

A True Story: What *Not* to Do

After being nicely cultivated by a key volunteer, I was asked to become a "keystone" supporter to a local organization. The cause is one I believe in and I was pleased to lend my support.

However, I counter-offered: instead of a one-time gift of $300 (the amount suggested by the solicitator), I was willing to commit to $50 a month for a year—$600 in total. I gave credit card authorization to begin the process with a first payment in March.

The following day I received a call from the organization's executive director thanking me for my generosity. She informed me that "ABC" deactivates its credit card process from April through October because "the campaign only runs from October through March."

Without asking my permission, they had charged my credit card for $300 (March through September payments on my pledge). It was *not* all right with me and my respect for "ABC" deteriorated as a result.

Is the above incident an isolated horror story? Unfortunately not. Too many not-for-profits consistently send messages that they view prospects as adversaries rather than partners. They ignore donors' requests for information, treat them as a faceless mass, and continue to offer obsolete fulfillment methods.

Educate everyone in your organization as to the benefits of donor retention. Notes William A. Sherden, in *Market Ownership: The Art & Science of Becoming #1*: "It is very costly to acquire new customers and put them on the books. In almost any industry, these one-time costs (both up-front and back-end if the client is lost) generally range from 2 to 4 times the annual cost of serving clients on an ongoing basis."

Following the above suggestions can make such a difference to your organization's well-being that it will make converts of the skeptical. *Just keep reminding everyone that a 5% increase in customer loy-*

alty can produce profit increases from 25 to 85%. And, the gains to your organization won't stop with current gift giving.

Creating "apostles" provides you with additional market penetration opportunities. In the next chapter we'll discuss the potential of planned giving as a donor product-expansion vehicle.

CHAPTER NINE

Donor Product Expansion through Planned Giving

> **Focus on your share of the prospect rather than on prospect share.**

THROUGH THE MID-1990s, fund raisers focused on acquiring larger and larger numbers of new donors. This made perfect sense with a growing (Boomer) adult population. *But now that our adult population has stabilized, a new paradigm must rule.*

Dr. Thomas Stanley, founder of The Affluent Institute and author of several books on reaching the individuals with high discretionary incomes, emphasizes the importance of "going deep rather than wide." In other words, focus on extending your product line to your current customer rather than finding a new prospect.

Thomas Gaffny and Richard Murdock, Epsilon creative execs, note that "today's strongest charities are like the strongest department stores—they offer their clientele a lot of options and choices."

Notes William A. Sherden, in *Market Ownership: The Art & Science of Becoming #1*:

"As customers gain trust in the company and in the value of its products, they become much more receptive to purchasing additional products . . . Cross-selling also has an impact on market affinity and customer relationships. In particular, customer retention improves with the number of product relationships the company has with the customer. Multiple-product relationships intensify the customer's involvement with the company and make it much more difficult to switch to one or more new providers."

The most underused cross-selling or product-expansion vehicle for fund raisers is planned giving. Though most development officers talk a good game about the importance of providing donors with information on bequests, life-income gifts, and the use of appreciated property, few shops commit the staffing and budget resources to do the job effectively. As a result, just *6% of Americans say they have bequests to charities in their wills.*

That's too bad. According to the National Committee on Planned Giving, few individuals ever change their wills to remove charitable bequests. It's almost "guaranteed" future income. And, because two-thirds of life gifts are for less than $25,000, most will be unrestricted income for your institution.

What institutions can benefit from planned gifts? The U.S. Trust Survey of Affluent Americans reveals that 49% of individuals with high discretionary incomes will leave at least some part of their estate to charity:

Academic institutions	to receive 58%
Health charities	45%
Religious institutions	34%
Public-policy and environmental organizations	24%
Libraries or museums	20%

There is a new focus on charitable donations and bequests outside the family. The results of a survey conducted by Price & Associates for the *Private Asset Management* newsletter indicate that nearly 85% of affluent people said they were highly inclined to be philanthropic. Fifty-seven percent indicated philanthropy was a significant part of their lives. Slightly more than half said they were actively involved in recruiting others to donate to their favorite causes.

The U.S. Trust Survey of Affluent Americans reveals that over 70% have taken steps to minimize estate taxes. Over half (54%) have established trusts and 40% are giving money away!

Philanthropy through planned gifts is on the rise. The probability of making bequests outside the traditional family increased from 19 to 29% between 1983 and 1991.

One-third of affluent people, a 37.4% rise over the previous year, say they created bequests, charitable remainder trusts, pooled income funds, and other planned gifts in 1993. Financial advisers indicate that their customers are increasingly interested in planned gifts because they like being able to make a financial commitment to an organization and thus obtain more generous tax benefits than they would get by making cash donations.

Two-thirds of all existing bequests have been established within the last 5 years. Perhaps, most importantly, donors like the fact that they do not have to part with a large amount of money at one time to make a planned gift.

With more and more people living into their 80s and 90s, public concerns about retirement income are increasing. In l960, only 1 American in 10 was age 65 or over. Today, that ratio is about 1 in 8, and it could reach 1 in 6 within 30 years. Americans age 85 and over have

---

As more of us live longer, our concerns grow in two areas:

- How will I fund my retirement?

- How will I cover end-of-life medical expenses?

Our conclusion may very well be:
Giving away assets during life, rather than at death, is foolish.

As a result, "ultimate" gifts—sacrificial gifts of assets during one's lifetime— will be made reluctantly, at best. Would *you* be willing to make a major gift in your 60s, knowing you had another 20, 30, or more years of living?

SOURCE: *Pinpointing Affluence: Increasing Your Share of Major Donor Dollars*, Judith E. Nichols, Precept Press, 1994

increased from 940,000 in 1960 to 3.1 million today and will reach 5.4 million in 2020.

One way to calm anxieties about retirement funds is annuities, one of the fastest-growing insurance products. One of New York Life's hot products is a single-premium retirement annuity. Also gaining popularity are policies that provide income to clients while they are alive. For example, one policy pays out retirement income while reserving a tax-free death payment to a beneficiary.

James Minehart leads development efforts at United Church Homes, a not-for-profit that has consistently done well with planned gifts from mature audiences. UCH has already shifted to the new paradigm, making personal contact and relationship building its priority. The donor base tends towards mature individuals—many elderly females. Jim notes that "United Church Homes' focus has been on getting our loyal, committed partners to focus on bequests and charitable gift annuities because these vehicles meet *our donors'* needs.

"Bequests allow donors to make larger gifts. They do not want to take the risk of needing public assistance nor of being unable to pay for medical and burial costs. And, charitable gift annuities offer the reassurance of a fixed income (and, the older the donor the higher the rate!). Our donors like those monthly checks. Many have renewed with a second annuity—it's an extension of the annual giving program."

United Church Homes also helps solve a big donor problem—asset appreciation.

"These donors purchased their assets years ago. I focus on fixing donor problems and they call *me* for advice."

Don't limit your marketing to traditional, mature audiences. More people under 45 (28%) than over 70 (22%) have made planned gifts!

- 22% of all charitable bequests were established by people over 70

- 20% were created by people between 60 and 69

- 30% from people between 45 to 59

- 28% were set up by those under 45

Planned Gifts Vary
by Donor Age

Age	Life Income	Non-Cash	Bequests
Less than 45	31%	22%	28%
45–59	22	30	30
60–69	21	25	20
70+	26	23	22

Source: National Committee on Planned Giving, 1994

Targeting Boomers and Busters
for Planned Giving

Why target Boomers and Busters for planned gifts?

- Changing family patterns affect wealth accumulation and distribution

Because many Boomers have had children later in life, what might have been several middle years of accumulation of retirement resources is now a time when the 19-year-old child of 55-year-old parents is starting college. Unlike their parents and grandparents, the fortysomething generation isn't necessarily looking to early retirement as a desirable goal.

In the next 20 years, $8 trillion to $10 trillion will pass from a senior generation (famous for making money and babies) to its children (Boomers). Two-thirds of upscale 30- to 59-year-olds expect to receive an inheritance—mostly in the form of real estate and/or money. Home equity constitutes the largest share of net worth: 43%. Interest-earning assets account for a large share, too: deposits at financial institutions make up 14%. Other interest-earning assets, such as money-market funds and municipal bonds, and IRA or KEOGH accounts, each constitute 4% of net worth. Stocks and mutual-fund shares account for 7%. The median value of inheritance is thought to be $135,000.

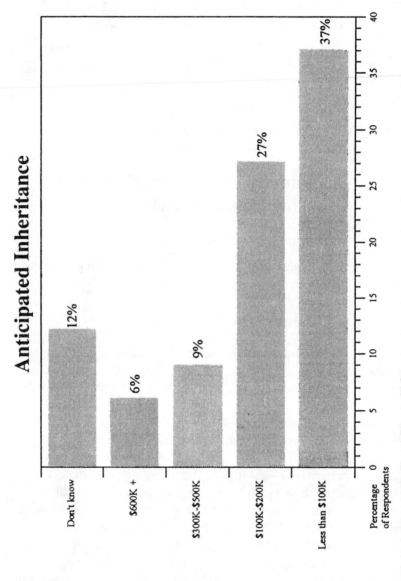

Anticipated Inheritance

Phoenix Home Life Fiscal Fitness℠ Survey
Conducted by Yankelovich Partners 1994

Few families have discussed the details of the wealth transfer—and that creates an exciting opportunity for our organizations because it does not appear that the inheritances are being counted on to make major changes in the lives of inheritors. In fact, for many, the money will create tax problems, coming just as they reach their highest income-earning years.

- Most younger and middle-aged adults are comfortable dealing with planned giving because they have grown up in a world where sophisticated financial planning is a mark of status.

Upscale 30- to 59-year-olds are very self-reliant when it comes to money management issues.

- The average age for preparing a will is 35. Yet just 60% of upscale 30- to 59-year-olds have made a will—less than half in their 30s and more than 3 out of 4 in their 50s. Most who have wills have not updated them in 5 years.

- They have not considered gifts or investments to offset estate taxes. Consideration increases among those in their 50s and those earning more than $100,000 per year. (Average current estate size is estimated to be $260,000 and this amount is expected to double by retirement.)

Both Boomers and Busters are taking long-term financial concerns seriously, according to the 1994 Equitable Nest Egg Study. The *primary* financial concern of both Boomers (32%) and Busters (29%) is funding their retirement. However, the study also reveals that most Boomers and Busters need to develop financial plans and sharpen their investment skills.

- **Financial Plans**: Only 52% of Boomers and 37% of Busters have developed a financial plan.

- **Insecure in Investing Skills**: Most Boomers and Busters rate their investment skills as average to below average.

Financial planners can help those seeking to plan for financial independence with a career-of-choice, rather than early retirement, as well as those concerned with more traditional retirement plans. This growing concern creates an opportunity for our organizations. Unlike their parents and grandparents, Boomers are suspicious of traditional financial advisors.

Targeting Women Prospects for Planned Giving

Why target women for planned gifts?

Women have money

- Because women outlive men by an average of 7 years, 89% of the wealth passes through their hands.

- Thirty-seven percent of all stock investments are owned by women.

- Single women comprise 35 million of the United States' 51 million stockholders.

- Female proprietorships are expected to reach 50% of all business ownership by 2000.

Women are into estate planning:

- The same proportion of men and women have made wills.

- Women, more than men, report having set up trusts.

Men and women are different:

Bequests by Men and Women Show Different Priorities		
	Men	**Women**
Education, medicine, science	26.0%	33.5%
Social welfare and other	22.1%	28.1%
Arts and humanities	2.1%	8.5%
Religious institutions	8.5%	11.9%
Private foundations	41.3%	18.0%
SOURCE: Internal Revenue Service		

A key difference between men and women is that women report more uncertainty on how to invest and less self-reliance in making financial decisions.

Women are just as optimistic as men about their financial future, but are often less comfortable in dealing with financial matters.

Many older women have minimal financial experience beyond handling the household budget. While women are definitely taking a more active role in managing finances, Jan Warner—a Columbia, South Carolina, lawyer who runs SoloSource Inc., a service that counsels divorced women on financial options—estimates that three-quarters of his female clients, most of whom are 40 or over, come to him without the financial know-how needed to make it alone comfortably.

"Midlife and older women often find themselves in very precarious positions when suddenly faced with death or divorce," says Barbara Hughes, a specialist with AARP's Women's Financial Information

Program. "They may have to make major financial decisions on investments, taxes, insurance, pensions, etc. in a very short period of time."

Even among working women in two executive-income households, wives are more likely to manage the day-to-day family finances, like balancing the checkbook and paying household bills, while the husband makes the investment and major financial decisions.

A Gallup study commissioned by New York Life shows that professional women need to pay more attention to their long-term financial futures. Although 82% of female executives initially called themselves "well-informed" about retirement planning, more than 72% of the 220 professional women polled turned out to be only "vaguely or not familiar" with fundamental investment concepts like compounding, inflation, and tax deferral, compared to 53% of the men surveyed. Women were also wary of taking on even minimal investment risks, with half the women preferring low-risk (and low-return) investments exclusively.

Most young women need to begin making plans for their retirement. Women in their 20s, 30s, and early 40s appear reluctant to think about planning for retirement. Yet, the overwhelming majority of women—82%—surveyed by Oppenheimer Management believe they will be solely responsible for their financial well-being at some point in their lives.

Setting up a
Planned-Giving Program

For most organizations, the notification of a charitable bequest comes as a surprise. That's because most organizations have never tracked bequests and other expectancies. They don't have a clue of who their planned-giving donors are!

Charitable institutions have not been notified of nearly three-quarters of all bequests and half of all life-income arrangements.

Success with a planned-giving program requires a long-term commitment. Not only must an organization accept that there is increasing competition from other not-for-profits for "ultimate" gifts, but there must be recognition that planned gifts are solicited in the present for the future. If the organization changes, is perceived differently, enters into a crisis, uses different staff and volunteers, and so on, the gift may be withdrawn or redefined.

Conventional thinking suggests it will take 3 to 5 years before an organization sees solid (i.e., dollar) returns from a planned-giving program. Your board and executive director must understand and accept that the steps being proposed in this report will start the "seeding" process, but cannot guarantee when the first gifts will be realized.

Planned-giving programs also require financial resources. The thrust of such programs is informational and educational. That requires a constant flow of brochures, flyers, inserts, newsletters, workshops, and visits.

A successful planned-giving program is the result of carefully coordinating ongoing vehicles to provide information, cultivation, and finally, solicitation. The three components do not necessarily exist linearly; rather, they overlap and must be done continuously.

A successful planned-giving program builds upon a foundation of interest and understanding among potential and existing constituencies so that an appeal for bequests and other planned gifts follows logically from ongoing communications.

1. Concentrate educational efforts on internal audiences—both as a whole and to targeted constituencies within—utilizing existing vehicles and putting new vehicles in place as needed.

2. In the case of the clients you serve, information to their families on handling long-term financial needs is a true service.

It is necessary to formulate an overall planned-giving strategy with general recommendations, specific action steps, and a time-line for implementation. This will provide your organization with the most efficient and effective program for planned giving.

- Offer internal seminars on financial planning

- Include columns on financial giving in your newsletters

- Use "targeted" newsletters

- Focus on payroll-deduction vehicles with staff

- Cultivate internal constituencies through service-milestone recognition, birthday cards, etc.

Here is an assortment of specifics to consider:

A. Develop a consistent statement to be included in all newsletters, volunteer resource guides, program brochures, etc. that invites the reader to consider making a "gift of significance" to your organization. Include coupons or reply devices as appropriate.

B. Develop an umbrella planned-giving brochure and reply vehicle to be used for follow-up to specific requests. Focus on case examples and stories rather than technical information

C. Identify one or two logical prospects for planned gifts. Work to get their commitments as charter members of your Leadership Heritage Society. Use their commitments to encourage others to explore the concept.

D. Create a Planned-Giving Resource Advisory Council. Encourage members of the financial community (trust officers, insurance agents, CPAs, realtors, financial planners, etc.) to view your organization as a resource for clients.

  - Encourage participants to follow up with individual clients who fit case example profiles.

  - Ask for financial advisors to volunteer services to your constituents seeking specific advice on making gifts. Develop a directory of participants.

By understanding what is happening in our society and how your organization's planned-giving program can serve as a resource to its constituents, you can have access to a greater share of each donor.

CHAPTER TEN

Reconnecting Lapsed Donors

Every lost donor costs you money and time. A key objective is to "reconnect"—to get people *back* to supporting your organization. To do so, you need to commit to using the best methods of communication.

Some FORMS OF communication carry more weight with donors and prospects than others. Direct forms, which allow for two-way communication, are best. Direct forms include face-to-face and telephone.

While face-to-face solicitation is, without doubt, the most effective way of getting more and larger gifts, it is also the most time-consuming and the hardest method to get volunteers to agree to do.

Most not-for-profits, faced with that reality, decide to use direct mail for the majority of their prospect base. *Before our paradigm shifted, this made sense.* Older Americans are, in fact, extremely responsive to direct mail. Unfortunately, direct mail has limited results with Busters and Boomers: younger individuals prefer face-to-face or telephone solicitations.

But, as Mal Warwick notes, "Many fund-raising managers dismiss telephone fund raising out-of-hand because of personal bias or resistance from board members."

He asserts that telephone fund raising is "especially cost-effective in reconnecting lapsed and former donors. A far larger percentage of

> **Response to phone appeals peaks in middle age:**
>
> - Typical outbound conversion rates from prospect to buyer are 6 to 8% versus 2% for direct mail, according to *Direct* magazine
>
> - Adding a phone call to your mail campaign can increase response rates by as much as 300%. The telephone call should be scheduled within 1 to 2 weeks, notes *DM News*

these individuals are likely to resume their support when contacted by phone than will respond to even the most effective letter. Sometimes even long-lapsed donors—those whose most recent gift was received 3 or more years ago—can be reactivated by telephone at break-even for the current campaign—and cultivated for later efforts."

Although many people insist they hate telephone solicitations —up to 60% of consumers say they won't listen to an unsolicited sales pitch on the telephone—**it works** . . . Ken Burnett, writing in *Relationship Fundraising*, reminds us: how many people get out of the bathtub to answer a letter?

Using Telecommunications: A Combined Direct Mail & Phone Strategy

Too many fund raisers think of telemarketing when they think of telephone fund raising. This method focuses on "dials per hour": getting on and off the phone as quickly as possible regardless of the impression left behind. It is *never* appropriate for your organization to use this methodology.

However, there is an alternative. By combining direct mail and phone contact, your organization can let a larger group of modest donors enjoy the sense that they are major donors, without incurring the heavy volunteer commitment such a campaign would require.

The combination of direct mail and phone contact also helps to introduce the concept of pledging, which will increase the dollar amount received and the fulfillment rate. Most current annual donors "self-identify" their level of giving, choosing a gift that feels comfortable.

The donor decides upon a "check commitment" level low enough not to cause any "stretching." In fact, it is often a gift that can be repeated several times a year. We can substantially increase modest donor income by educating the under-$100 donor to make his or her chosen level gift more often. Our initial goal might be to ask for four payments of the "check commitment amount."

Results:

1. Depending on target audiences chosen, monies raised will be significantly higher both in terms of the total dollars raised and the dollars committed per prospect. (Non-donor prospects often achieve a pledge rate of 35%.)

2. Fulfillment (as opposed to pledge rate) will be also significantly higher, especially among those who choose to make a multi-period pledge rather than a one-time gift. (Fulfillment rates as high as 98% have been confirmed.)

3. Cost per dollar raised will be significantly lower than for direct mail or phone contact alone. Typically, costs for a direct mail/phone contact program will be 17 to 33 cents per dollar raised. (Programs which concentrate on current and previous donors have costs as low as 4 cents per dollar raised.)

Direct mail/phone contact programs can be done on-site by the organization using either paid callers or volunteers, or through contracting with a vendor. On-site programs tend to do slightly better because of the ambience and caller's closer feelings to the organization; but this needs to be balanced against space requirements.

Pre-approach letters set the stage for the fulfillment phone call. They present the full case for support and suggest an appropriate level of giving for each prospect. Within two weeks, your prospects should receive a fulfillment phone call. The positioning is unique: callers are not soliciting, but rather helping the prospect come to a decision. This is more acceptable to both caller and prospect.

However the calls are made (on-site or by an outside vendor), a key to the success of the program is creating a relaxed atmosphere where the caller respects the prospect's need to consider his or her options and the prospect believes he or she will make a difference to the organization. Because callers are trained to believe that they are communicators rather than salespersons, the ambience of the calling room is not that of a high-pressure telephone center.

On the following pages, you will find a sample phone-contact script that can be easily modified to fit the needs of your organization.

Phone Contact Script for ABC Phonathon Callers

Thank you for your willingness to make a limited number of follow-up calls to our "family"—individuals who volunteer to our organization. In the past, these individuals also donated to ABC, but we have not received a gift in over a year.

Our goal is two-fold:

1. to thank these individuals for their generous support of time and effort,

   and

2. to encourage them to consider making a fiscal year gift at this time.

Each individual you are contacting has already received a letter from Ms. X, president of our organization, asking him or her to consider renewing his or her support. You are helping the prospect make the decision to meet (or not meet) the request by answering any questions he or she has regarding making the gift.

All materials (letter, leadership gift club brochure, reply envelope) educate individuals that *"It costs $100 to support 1 child in ABC Organization's after-school program for 1 year."* For those who are able, we ask that they consider making a gift at this level, payable as $25 quarterly or $9 monthly.

Your goal is to make them feel appreciated, not pressured, in considering their ongoing support of the goals and objectives served by the ABC Organization.

When contacting prospective donors, ask to speak with the prospect by name, identifying yourself as "Mary/John Smith, a supporter of the ABC Organization, calling on behalf of Ms. X, president.

Telephone Tips

Use the correct introduction:
> say your name and organizational affiliation slowly, loudly, and very distinctly. People who say their name clearly do not appear to have anything to hide. This small gesture builds great trust.

Use the listener's name at least 3 times in the first 10 seconds of the opening statement.

Create a dialog: ask questions; pause for answers

If prospect is available

a. Re-identify yourself when the prospect gets on phone: "Mr./Ms. Jones, I am Mary/John Smith, a long time friend of the ABC Organization, calling on behalf of Ms. X, president."

b. Thank the prospect:
"First and foremost, I want to let you know how much the ABC Organization appreciates your support. The time and effort you give as a volunteer is the most generous gift of all."

c. Introduce the purpose of the call:
"I know Ms. X has asked you to consider a very special gift for the coming year. Would you consider making your gift at this time?"

d. Pause, listen, do not interrupt. Give her/him at least seven seconds of silence!

e. Respond based on what is said by the prospect.

If your prospect has a complaint:

- Listen without interrupting.

- Do not argue.

- Restate the concern.

- Ask what he or she would like to see happen.

- Resolve the concern if you are able to, or indicate that it will be promptly referred to Ms. X and the prospect will receive a call-back tomorrow during the daytime if that is convenient.

Agree with your prospect if he or she indicates it is a change from last year.

Emphasize what the gift will accomplish: "With your help, we can . . ."

f. Ask again if you have not received a definitive "yes" or "no."

"Will you consider becoming a 19— member of the ABC Leadership Society with your gift of $100, payable as a one-time gift, $25 quarterly, or $9 monthly?"

g. Pause again, listen, do not interrupt.

If prospect indicates a gift at the amount requested:

1. Thank him or her.

2. Confirm the timing/method of payment.

3. Double-check the address and indicate you will send a confirming letter and reply envelope.

If prospect says no:

1. Do not argue. Emphasize how much his or her past support is appreciated.

2. Ask if you might get back in contact later.

3. Thank the prospect for his or her time.

End all conversations by indicating, again, the sincere thanks of the ABC organization for the donor's continuing support.

If prospect is not available:

- Ask when a good time is to call back and indicate that you will do so. Say thank you and end the conversation.

Seven out of ten times, the person you're calling won't be available.

Even worse, when the person returns your call, there's only a 30% chance you'll be available.

1. Plan a brief message before dialing.

2. Always have your message read back to you.

3. Try to get an idea of when your call will be returned.

4. Use an alarm to remind yourself to return calls.

5. Leave a "good news" message: name, phone number, and a little information about why you're calling.

6. Ask if anyone else can help you.

7. Arrange "phone appointments" with specific times for you to call again.

SOURCE: Nancy Friedman, president, Telephone Doctor, St. Louis.

CHAPTER ELEVEN

Selectively Acquiring New Donors: Affluent Segments

> **All donors *are not* equal. Acquire only the donors you want: those who give enough and with flexibility.**

BECAUSE NOT EVERYONE is philanthropic, a useful starting place is to know, at least generally, who gives. According to a survey conducted by the Barna Group, most donors are likely to:

- be female (55%)

- have attended college (58%)

- be currently married (63%)

- not have children under 18 presently living in their home (61%)

- be white (78%)

- live in an urban area (54%)

- be affiliated with a major political party (72%)

- live in a household with an aggregate annual pre-tax income of more than $25,000 (72%)

If you're willing to accept gifts at any level (usually low rather than high), that's all the information you need. But that approach is unfortunate. **Most not-for-profits let their donors choose them, rather than choosing their donors.** As a result, two equally problematic results often occur:

1. Your loyal core of donors give as generously as their means allow, but it's not enough to meet your organization's needs.

2. You receive "fair share," token gifts from those capable of doing much more.

When not-for-profits realize they're in this situation, what do they do? Often, they decide it's time to launch a major gifts program and go after the mega-gifts. Makes sense—or does it?

Be careful. You may be creating more problems than solutions:

• The wealthy are a small group and are known to everyone in your community. Unless there is prior history of interest in the organization, cultivation is a long, slow process.

• Large gifts tend to be restricted gifts. Few people hand over amounts greater than $10,000 without wanting to know, very specifically, how the dollars will be used.

It may be a good time to stop fantasizing about those million-dollar gifts and focus your fund raising on affluent donors capable of giving annual gifts of $1,000 and greater.

The truth is that less than 400 gifts from individuals at the $1 million-plus level are reported by Giving USA each year from the pool of 4 million Americans who qualify as millionaires. Approximately 300 additional mega-gifts are added by corporate and foundation giving, bringing the grand total still far short of 1,000.

On the other hand, there are 29 million Americans with discretionary income. All households with incomes of over $50,000 have discretionary income. Those earning more than $80,000 have more than $11,000 a year to spend on leisure, charity, and other nonessential purchases.

Most exciting, according to Dr. Thomas Stanley, head of The Affluent Market Institute, is that "the affluent population, whether measured in terms of a minimum annual household income of $100,000 or

a net worth of $1 million or more, is far outpacing the growth of the household population."

And, being philanthropic is important to affluents. According to a *Town and Country* magazine/Roper Starch survey of individuals with household incomes of $100,000 or more, being a trustee of a cultural or educational institution (62%) edges out even being a top executive of a large corporation or owning one's own business (61% each) as the top symbol of status or achievement among affluents!*

It's time to get real. *Not only are most not-for-profits not positioned to find million-dollar donors, but many organizations don't really want the restricted gifts that most major donors insist on giving.*

So, if you're looking to acquire new donors capable of giving significant unrestricted funding for the operating budget, think affluence instead of wealth!

Redefine Who is a Major Donor

Stop thinking of major donors in terms of gifts or assets. **The average millionaire** is a white male business owner, 57 years old, with 2 kids, who works 10 to 14 hours a day, 6 days a week. He earns about $120,000 a year. Notes Dr. Thomas Stanley, in *Marketing to the Affluent*, "That's 4 or 5 times what the average family brings in, but it's not megabucks." And, 80% of the wealthy are first-generation millionaires, understandably cautious in making sacrificial gifts. Neither they nor the majority of our affluent prospects are able—or willing—to strip themselves of assets to make gifts of 5 figures.

Instead of "ultimate" gifts, think more boldly about annual gifts. **Look for prospects who can—and will—make regular yearly gifts of $1,000 to $100,000.** While only 1% of American individuals number themselves among the upper class, 14% are upscale households—more than 19 million households. Half of these upscalers have incomes higher than $66,000 and 15% (about 4 million households) have incomes greater than $100,000. In addition, there are about 1.5 million households with a net worth of over $1 million.

While finding the affluent requires more diligent searching,

---

*The survey results do not add up to 100% because multiple responses were given.

most of the names can be located. Education is the common thread. According to Judith Waldrop and Linda Jocobsen, writing in *American Demographics*, "In the 1990s, education and income go together like wine and cheese." The more education, the higher the earnings. Average monthly earnings range from $492 for adults without a high school diploma to $4,961 for holders of professional degrees. Increasing numbers of people are getting those bigger paychecks: in 1990, 25% of adults had earned a degree of some kind beyond high school, up from 21% in 1984.

The most affluent counties in America are also among the best-educated. In Fairfax County, Virginia, with an affluence level nearly 6 times that of the rest of the United States, 42% of adults 25 and over are college graduates, compared with only 20% of all Americans that age. Seventy-four percent of all adults have gone to college; the median household income is $59,000; and more than half of the workers are managers, professionals, or technicians.

The single largest source of wealth creation in the world is entrepreneurial activity. Approximately 80% of the millionaires in this country work for a living. And 80% of these own their own businesses.

Six out of 10 of the truly affluent own their own businesses.

Notes *Working Woman* magazine, "In the 1960s there was a total of perhaps 7 or 8 million companies in the country—200,000 new annually. In 1989 we have a total of 19 million companies, with roughly 1 million start-ups last year alone. By 2000 we're going to have 30 million enterprises."

Who are today's small-business owners? They're young, averaging 38 years old: about 85% of all men and 78% of all women are self-employed before age 40. Fifty-six percent of all new businesses are formed by people between 25 and 40 years of age with the 30 to 34 age group the single most productive 5-year interval. Money is not the biggest attraction to owning their own businesses: most are concerned, rather, about issues of independence and power.

Next to business owners and self-employed professionals, sales and marketing professionals are your best prospects. The growth of incentive compensation for employees has created strong pockets of affluence. As more and more smaller and mid-sized businesses offer substantial bonuses to employees who perform, many younger sales people—especially in high-tech industries—are receiving single large payments. Because people who are compensated this way, as opposed to receiving steady payments throughout the year, are more likely to save all or part of the windfall, they may be ideal prospects for significant gifts—especially if you help them with financial planning.

Generally, more Americans than ever before are thinking "charitably." According to a Grey Advertising survey, a powerful wave of soul-searching and uncertainty has swept across this country, bringing dramatic, long-term changes to the marketplace.

Many Americans—people who believed and behaved as if abundance would never end —are now, in many cases for the first time, coming to grips with limitations. Today, Americans are experiencing doubts about their collective and individual futures. In recognizing those fears and doubts, Americans have moved from an attitude of invincibility to a deep and unsettling sense of vulnerability.

Expanding the Giving Base: Attracting New Donors

- Non-white donors, while giving to fewer charities overall, are more likely to try new organizations.

- Donors in the South and Northeast U.S. are most likely to give to new organizations.

Source: Based on a survey by NPT/Barna Research

As a result: Americans are putting a new emphasis on human relations. The desire for a sense of belonging extends right out the front door and into the community: 90% of Americans believe we should do more to help the homeless, and 87% are now "more interested in playing a role in protecting the environment."

In order to attract affluent donors you need to understand their demographics and psychographics. Chapter 12 focuses on understanding the prospect pool of today's and tomorrow's donors: mature individuals, maturing Boomers and the young adult market of Busters and Boomlets.

A full treatment of the material in this chapter can be found in my book, *Pinpointing Affluence: Increasing your share of major donor dollars* (Precept Press, 1993).

CHAPTER TWELVE

Understanding the Prospect Pool of Today's and Tomorrow's Donors

> **Individuals of all ages are thinking "charitably."**
> Sixty-three percent of persons age 45 to 59 and 59% of those over 60 donate. Surprisingly, middle-aging Boomers—thought of as a selfish generation—give more than their proportionate share to charity. Sixty-five percent of Boomers are likely to make charitable contributions.

Today's Best Donors: Mature Individuals

IN CASE YOU haven't noticed, the world is turning gray. During the past 2 decades, the number of persons 45 and over increased almost 30% more than the rest of the population. Whether we look at population trends in America, Canada, the United Kingdom, France, Germany, Italy, the Scandinavian countries, or Japan, the implication is clear: Our countries will never again be societies of youth.

Not only are people living longer, but the demographics of the aging Boomer "hump" (those born from 1946 to 1964), plus the lowering of the birth rate, guarantees that older individuals will, increasingly, be the focus of our populations.

In the U.S., when the century closes, there will be 31 million people over 65, comprising more than 12% of the population. And before the Baby Boom is finished, there will be 55 million people over 65, amounting to 18% of the population.

Similar statistics are found in developed countries around the globe. In 1951, only 28% of the U.K. population were "grays"; in 1994, this figure stands at 31.3% (about 18 million individuals); by 2024 it will have risen to 40.2% (about 23.5 million). By then, some observers claim, nearly half of all British adults will be 50 or over.

How Well Off are Mature Individuals?

People over 50 control much of a nation's wealth. They control half of America's discretionary income (though they are not quick to spend it) and 77% of America's assets, including more than 70% of all money market accounts and certificates of deposit. Seven out of ten own their homes (with the median value of a single-family home rising from $23,000 to $89,300 between 1970 and 1988), and 80% of those are without a mortgage. Half of all American millionaires fall into this group.

Mature individuals are our most philanthropic audience. Mature households contribute to charitable causes 13% more than the average household. Currently, they contribute more than average to religious organizations, charities, and political candidates, in that order, but less than average to educational institutions. They tend to listen to society's recommendations and like to support traditional charities such as United Way.

Who are Today's Mature Individuals?

Psychographically, mature individuals generally fall into two groupings:

Depression Babies: individuals born prior to 1939 have "civic" personalities—believing it is the role of the citizen to fit into society and make it better. They believe in "the American Way," "making the world safe for democracy," and, seeing themselves as leaders, are strong volunteers and contributors. Always mindful of the lessons of their childhood, their money personalities are conservative. It is hard for them to part with significant dollars no matter how comfortable they are economically.

World War II Babies: born from 1940 to 1945, this smaller group of individuals was taught to be "silent," conforming to the will of the group rather than their own individuality. They were taught to "earn" their way in society and volunteer and give because that's "the right thing to do." Their parents drilled the lessons of the Great Depression into them, but "Silents" reached adulthood in the golden economic days of the late 1950s through early 1970s, benefitting from real estate appreciation, a booming stock market, portable pensions, government entitlements, and inflation. Now in early retirement, many are willing to spend on themselves if not on charity.

Older individuals still remember when modest dollars had major muscle. For both groups, annual gift-giving is often pegged at $25 (or its equivalent). It can be very difficult to upgrade contributions.

And, with life expectancies stretching out, both mature groups have a real fear of outliving assets. Therefore, many will make their major gifts through bequests rather than current giving. Both Depression and World War II Babies tend to distrust newer technologies. They prefer outright gifts to pledges, cash to credit cards, and rarely use electronic fund transfer in making contributions.

Marketing to Affluent Older Individuals

Avoiding negative myths: A major problem in marketing to older individuals is that our culture is deeply "gerontophobic." Ken Dychtwald, author of *AgeWave*, notes that "We have a fear of aging and a prejudice against the old that clouds all our perceptions about what it means to grow old."

Dychtwald identifies six prevalent negative myths and stereotypes that blind us:

Myth 1: People over 65 are old.

Myth 2: Most older people are in poor health.

Myth 3: Older minds are not as bright as young minds.

Myth 4: Older people are unproductive.

Myth 5: Older people are unattractive and sexless.

Myth 6: All older people are pretty much the same.

> The key to reaching older individuals is to market positively.

More frequent communications are the key to keeping and upgrading your older prospects. Use longer letters, case examples, and testimonials. Provide facts and figures along with a narrative. Be prepared to follow up with phone calls. Be sure to increase type size in your communication vehicles; after age 40, eyes can use some help! Remember, a person who begins giving to you in his or her 50s may live to be 90. A yearly gift of $25 for 40 years is $2,000—a major donor!

Use appropriate role models. Mature individuals are attractive. Use photographs that emphasize vitality. Show older adults in active situations. Robert B. Maxwell, American Association of Retired Persons vice president, notes that while the young are getting older, "the old are getting younger. The 70-year-old today is more like 50-year-old of 20 years ago. We have not yet found the fountain of youth, but research has shown that healthy older people can enjoy most of their mental and physical abilities and even improve on them."

Use appeals that leave autonomy and independence intact. Use the term "older individuals," "mature individuals," or "aging" as opposed to "elderly" or "senior citizens." And say "50 years or over" rather than "or older." Position your planned-giving appeals to discuss financial well-being. Portray the concerns of older persons in a positive light.

Respect their preferences. Many older persons do not like traveling at night. The Portland Home and Garden Show traditionally opened at 6 P.M. on a Thursday. In 1988, when the opening hour was set at 11 A.M., attendance went up 1,500 over the same Thursday the previous year. Older attendees made the difference.

Recognize that life goes on. Even when older persons are not married, many enjoy active relationships. Be careful to include "the significant other" in discussions and invitations. Romance at later ages also brings with it concerns for protecting assets. Sensitive financial planning advice may be welcome by the entire family.

Market in appropriate publications. Most communities have a local seniors paper. Read it regularly and offer to contribute articles on your organization.

Aged to Perfection

Middle-aged and older consumers respond
to more personalized messages.

Mature Adults	Young Adults
Declining influence by peers	Heavily influenced by peers
Declining material values	Highly materialistic values
More subjective	More objective
More introspective	More extrospective
High sensitivity to context	Low sensitivity to context
Perceptions in shades of gray	Perceptions in black and white
More flexible	More rigid
More individualistic	More subordinated to others
More discretionary behavior	More predictable behavior
Less price sensitive	More price sensitive
Complex ways of determining values	Simple ways of determining values
Whole-picture oriented	Detail oriented

Source: "Serving the Ageless Market," David Wolfe, *American Demographics*, 1994

Understand that mature individuals are different, psycho-graphically, from younger adults. Compared to Boomers, they are more likely to cite declining influence by peers; have declining material values; consider themselves to be more subjective and introspective; are more sensitive to context; perceive "shades of gray"; are more flexible in their thinking and behavior; require a more individualistic approach; and bring a more complex way to determine values!

Differentiate between mature individuals. Consider segmenting your older donors and prospects:

- **INOYs: I'm-Not-Old Yets   50 to 70 years of age**
  - are often "in transition," not fully retired
  - like volunteer activities that affirm their experience and expertise
  - may be fearful of spending; not sure of income/expenses
  - conditioned to marketing

- **OMBOKs: Old-May-Be Oks   70 to 90 years of age**
  - often "downsizing" activities and responsibilities
  - like volunteer activities with regular, dependable day-time schedules
  - have highest discretionary income, lowest expenses
  - lived through dramatic change in own adult lives; distrustful of direct mail

- **TOP: Top-of-the-Population   over 90 years of age**
  - fastest growing segment, much less mobile
  - volunteering can counter isolation
  - highest assets; fearful of medical costs
  - likes direct mail; trusts your correspondence

Today and tomorrow, mature donors will continue to be our greatest resources for both contributions and volunteerism. Understanding them, demographically and psychographically, will help you reach older individuals more effectively.

Tomorrow's Best Prospects: Baby Boomers

As we move through the 1990s and into the twenty-first century, most not-for-profits must target Baby Boomers—that large adult grouping of individuals born from 1946 to 1964—as new and renewing donors.

The reason: the bulk of our population growth will occur because people are living longer, rather than because more people are being born. Your contributors tomorrow will be those individuals you attract today!

And, because Boomers are the most highly educated generation in history (48% of American Boomers have either attended or graduated from college) we can look forward to a continuing ground swell of affluence as they continue their careers.

Baby Boomers are capable of giving money. Boomers are just entering their peak earning years and will cause the number of affluent households to inflate to unprecedented heights. In the United States, the number of Boomers with the highest annual incomes ($75,000 and over) will increase from 2.2. million to 6.2 million, accounting for 1 in 7 households in this age group by the turn of the century.

They are accumulating wealth through property ownership, investment, and inheritance. In the U.S., over the next 20 years, $6.8 trillion to $8 trillion will be passed on to Boomers from parents and grandparents. Because these inheritances will occur in midlife (the highest income-earning years), many inheritees will look for ways to use the money in "nonessential" ways. Charitable giving may be high on the list for many.

Before you design a fund-raising plan targeting Boomers, you need to understand and accept that these prospects—and their giving habits—are dramatically different from individuals born before World War II.

Do you personally remember the Great Depression? The majority of adults in the world today were born after World War II, not before. The most significant grouping is the Baby Boom. Those born from 1946 to 1964 are the largest generational cohorts our society has ever had. *Today, Boomers form more than half the adult population in developed nations*. This is your target for current and future giving.

Not surprisingly, most people form their core values with regard to how they relate to money during the influential years when they first start working. This makes Boomers significantly different from their parents and grandparents, the donors we have been cultivating and soliciting since the 1960s.

Baby Boomers anticipate higher costs for everything, from cars to contributions. Boomers were fully immersed as consumers in the free-spending, affluent decades following World War II, try as their parents (and grandparents) did to inculcate in them a sense of financial practicality. Their point of view about money is thus somewhat different from that of their parents and is totally at odds with that of their grandparents. Essentially, their attitude is this: "If you have no money in the bank, but have at least 2 credit cards that aren't over the limit, you're doing fine."

Are Boomers Philanthropic?

Overwhelmingly, yes. Raised as "idealists," Boomers have been taught to put others ahead of themselves. They see themselves as "changing the world," not fitting in with it like their "civic" and "silent" parents and grandparents.

As they mature, Boomers are demonstrating a commitment to philanthropy that outpaces that of other age groups. In 1992, more Boomers gave to nonreligious charities than did people in any other age group, according to the Roper Organization. A survey by the Gallup Organization for Independent Sector projects that Boomer donations in the United States will increase from $361 million in 1985 to $387 million by 2000—contradicting the view that members of this generation are selfish or unwilling to financially support causes or institutions.

Baby Boomers are willing to give. In the years ahead, quality of life issues—making the world a better place for themselves and their children—will be the main preoccupation of Boomers. Few Boomers believe income dollars alone will improve their lifestyles. They know the problems are greater than one individual or one household.

Boomers want to make a difference. They know you can't save the world without spending big dollars. Asked properly, these younger, newer donors will gladly give larger, unrestricted gifts than did previous generations.

How Can We Get Boomers to Give?

Donor loyalty is not the Boomer norm: the annual donor that organizations counted on year after year for modest but steady giving has all but vanished as Baby Boomers seek out this year's "sexiest" causes.

Boomers have more choices in charities than earlier generations (nearly two-thirds of today's not-for-profits were created after 1946) and have shown less allegiance than their parents and grandparents display.

The heart of the dilemma is that Boomers view themselves as special people. Having been told they were unique from early childhood, Boomers:

- expect organizations seeking their patronage to cultivate them extensively even when they are contributing at modest levels;

- prefer to make contributions on a major scale, yet won't or can't commit to the cost up front.

To create donor loyalty in Boomers, concentrate on getting ongoing pledges rather than a single, larger gift. The monthly payment is the ultimate involvement device. It helps Boomers buy into your organization and helps you to identify them for recognition and extra cultivation.

Equally important, monthly payments break the psychological barrier. It enables the Boomer to make a gift at an enhanced level that reflects his or her "apartness from the crowd."

Understand Boomer "triggers":

- Instant gratification: recognize all gifts immediately.

- Increased accountability: Boomers don't trust anyone.

- Longer decision-making cycles: Boomers want more information.

- A focus on planned instead of major giving: with longer life expectancies, Boomers are unlikely to let go of assets.

Rethink your fund-raising strategies:

- Annual Giving: Ask for money at a level that reinforces a Boomer's sense of what will make a difference—a minimum request of $100. Don't confuse what the Boomer wants to do with how he or she can do it: the first is motivation; the second is fulfillment.

- Major Giving: Redefine your concept of a major donor to acknowledge cumulative as well as annual gifts. Remember, a 40-year-old donor, making an annual gift of $100, will give you $5,000 by the time he or she is 90.

- Planned Giving: Use single- and/or limited-premium insurance policies to allow Boomers to make a major gift to your organization now. Concentrate on Boomer concerns in marketing life-income gifts: retirement, aging parents, and college costs for children.

Know where to look for affluent Boomers. Unlike their parents, Boomers are less likely to be employees of large corporations.

The most successful Boomers tend to be entrepreneurs. Boomers cluster in urban environments rather than rural areas or suburbs, with the top ten U.S. cities being Houston; Denver; Washington, DC; Atlanta; San Francisco; Dallas; Albuquerque; Salt Lake City; Baton Rouge; and Portland, OR.

Remember that within a few years, the only donors and prospects we will have will be Boomers and younger adults. It makes sense to use the next five years to carefully plan a transition from our traditional mature donors to the very different Boomer audience.

Meet the Future: Busters and Boomlets

When we think of prospect groups, it's easy to ignore young adults and children. But these groups are very important to fund raisers:

- They significantly influence their parents' philanthropic choices.

- They have large amounts of discretionary income of their own.

- They are highly philanthropic.

- They are your only prospects for the twenty-first century.

The younger generational cohorts differ dramatically in their

attitudes, values, and lifestyles from their older brothers and sisters, parents, and grandparents.

Baby Busters: the 33 million "reactive" Americans born from 1965 to 1977 are the first generation of Americans to distrust the American Dream. They don't believe life will be better for them than their parents and see their role in life as pragmatic. They want to fix, rather than change.

Although the economic situation is more pessimistic for Busters than previous generations, many have high discretionary incomes: a combination of their continuing support by parents, postponing marriage and children, and a reordering of personal priorities. America's young adults and youth control $200 billion, mostly in discretionary dollars.

Following the much-heralded Boom, Busters could do nothing right. They were the throwaway children of divorce and poverty, the latchkey kids. Busters weren't trusted, nor appreciated, as youth and they carry the scars into adulthood. They are the most Republican-leaning youths of the twentieth century. Unlike Baby Boomers, Busters grew up in relative obscurity under television's supervising eye. Ignored or vilified by the media, they tend to be cautious, anti-intellectual, and pessimistic; many are fearful, frustrated, angry, and believe they will be exterminated in a nuclear war.

The myth of "Generation X"

Only 31% of Americans between 18 and 29, roughly 3 in 10, believe they share a common generation. And, of those who consider themselves part of a specific generation, only 10% prefer to think of themselves as Generation X. Today's 18- to 29-year-olds are one of the most diverse generations of Americans in ethnicity, education, and aspirations. They are the results of a culture of choice.

In fact, Busters have been given poor press. Today's 18- to 29-year-olds are generally no more—or less—cynical about the nation than all Americans. And, especially among college-educated 18- to 29-year-olds, they are fairly optimistic about their personal prospects.

Comparing aspects of their lives to their parents' at the same age, finds Busters a mixed bag. According to the Roper 18/29 syndicated report on the attitudes and behaviors of Americans 18- to 29-years-old: 50% of 18- to 29-year-olds think they have more fun than their parents did at the same age; but 56% think they have more stress than their parents did; just 36% think they're enjoying more financial success; only 24% think they have a happier family life; 21% think they're wiser; and 28% say they're working harder.

Generally, Busters are more optimistic than their elders about their personal prospects, though they are less optimistic than Boomers were at their age. *The top self-descriptors of Generation X*: fun (88%), outgoing (86%), and sociable (79%). At the bottom of the list are caring (49%), independent (41%), and value-conscious (39%).

They aspire to the traditional values of career, home, and family. While, on one hand, they are even more accepting of dual-career marriages than Boomers, Busters are also more inclined to plan to have larger families than did the Baby Boomers.

Busters are pragmatic idealists. They will need convincing proof that your organization is reliable and will simplify, rather than complicate their lives. Younger Americans are likely to look for more "personal" charities and to dislike workplace giving. They are more participatory in personality style, supporting only the organizations they actively work with.

Research shows Busters are more conservative than previous generations. They appear to have little interest in championing causes. Unlike the confrontational Boomers, Busters are more likely to negotiate and collaborate than to demonstrate. They enlist the aid of legislators to the causes they espouse. And, having been raised in an era of rapidly expanding communications technology, many are very sophisticated about attracting press attention.

Preferred message style: blunt and kinetic, with an appeal to brash survivalism. "I want us to be the generation that leads, that votes, that earns, that spends, that doesn't continue to let our parents fight our wars for us," notes Nicholas W. Nyhan, graduating senior, in a commencement speech at the University of Massachusetts at Amherst.

Financial style: twentysomethings have a different view of the American dream. Only 21% say the most important measure of living the good life is financial success; a scant 4% believe the criterion is owning a home. The rest are more concerned with the acquisition of intangibles: a rich family or spiritual life, a rewarding job, the chance to help others, and the opportunity for leisure and travel or for intellectual and creative enrichment.

Key life events: the crumbling of the Berlin Wall and opening of Eastern Europe.

Busters will give. They are the first generation not to equate success strictly in terms of material possessions. "Quality of life" issues will predominate for them—and probably for Boomlets as well. This bodes well for volunteerism and philanthropy. Concerns for the environment, parenting, and positive self issues, as well as continuing education, are priorities.

Philanthropy and spirituality are very important to a majority of teens. Research conducted at Teenage Research Unlimited suggests that Beavis and Butthead are not role models for today's youth. The share of teens who agree with the statement, "It's very important to me to get involved in things and help make the world better" increased from 65% in 1989 to 69% in 1992, then fell to 63% in 1993. Those who say their religion or faith is one of the most iportant parts of their lives increased from 53% in 1989 to 58% in 1992, then fell back to 53% in 1993.

Busters are making it clear they distrust workplace giving and have given rise to a whole generation of new charities: more personal in nature than those their parents and grandparents founded and supported. Busters are quite philanthropic, but see themselves as having only small amounts of disposable cash (their priorities include sharing with a large extended family of friends and colleagues) to give to charity. Their gift fulfillment needs to be structured to allow for a constant stream of extremely modest gift amounts.

Remember that younger persons grew up in a different world. Highly computer literate, they prefer the cashless society: using credit cards, standing bank drafts, and electronic transfers. An increased use of electronic newsletters, videos, e-mail and computer bulletin boards should be in your organization's future. Already 1.3 million Americans have used Prodigy for philanthropy. The computer network program allows people to look at information about the economic status of young children, take a brief quiz, and send for information on charities that work with children.

Meet the "Echo" Boom

Baby Boomlet: the 45 million-plus "civic" children of Boomers were born from 1978 through 1996, roughly following the ending of Boomers' child-bearing years. Now through age 16, Boomlets are currently 25% of the population. Before it ends in 1995, the boomlet may produce as many as 72 million Americans before continuing as the "echo bust."

Boomlets repeat the cycle of their grandparents. They will believe in science and cooperation and will be easily persuaded that theirs is a good and special group which knows how to build big things together. Society loves them: considering them smarter, better-behaved, and more civic-spirited that the Busters. This is the "smoke-free, drug-free class of 2000." They have heavy influence on parents and relatives, encouraging families to recycle and re-examine values.

Boomlets are growing up in a world without boundaries and are likely to extend their philanthropy well past their own country. Preferred message style: rational and constructive, with an undertone of optimism.

We will also be dealing with an increasingly culturally and ethnically diverse base of Boomlet prospects. In 1995, 63% of births will be to non-Hispanic white women. By 2050, the share could decrease to 41%. Blacks and Native Americans will only slightly increase their share of births. The share of Asian-American births will increase from 4% to 9% by 2050, while the share of Hispanic-origin births will rise from 16 to 29%. By 2010, 1 of every 3 children will be either non-white or Hispanic.

Minorities will exert more influence over the national agenda as the population of African Americans, Hispanics, and Asian Americans increases from 17% in 1990 to 33% by 2000. One of six workers belonged to an ethnic minority in 1990. By 2000, they will be 1 in 3. Not-for-profits need to learn how to be inclusive with these increasingly diverse client populations, volunteers, boards, and donors.

Because your younger audiences are the only prospects for the future and because they have such influence on their parents and grandparents, working with them now will have big dividends for your organization.

PART FOUR

Putting It All Together

Some organizations do it right. They build their organizations on a strong foundation of the basics *and* they use the elements of aftermarketing to renew, upgrade, and create core loyalty among their donors.

Chapters 13, 14 and 15 are case studies of fund-raising programs that have successfully used aftermarketing strategies to move their donors along:

Chapter 13, "Case Example: Aftermarketing with the Columbia River Girl Scout Council," explores how this Oregon-based not-for-profit uses an aftermarketing matrix to track communications with its donors. Included is a sample of the donor survey the Council has developed to learn more about its supporters' demographics and psychographics.

Chapter 14, "Case Example: UNICEF: Renewal and Upgrading," is a narrative of how the United States Committee for UNICEF moved my own giving from a first gift to a bequest commitment.

Chapter 15, "Case Example: Greenpeace Frontline: A Committed Giving Scheme," describes how the Frontline membership program generates nearly a million British pounds a year for that organization.

Their stories are exciting because *you* can do the same. As we end *Growing from Good to Great*, I urge you to draw inspiration from these organizations.

Finally, to succeed you need to set goals. Chapter 16 demonstrates how you can arrive at realistic, yet challenging targets for your organization's fund-raising programs.

Above all, remember that:

- Fund raising is a three-stage process: First, donors are acquired. Then, they are converted into repeat donors. Finally, donors may be upgraded into higher levels of generosity and commitment.

- We need to raise money from believers: Joan Flanagan, writing in *The Grass Roots Fundraising Book*, recommends asking "who wants what we do?" Find the people who believe in the purpose of your organization and who want you to succeed. Then, focus your efforts on connecting them.

CHAPTER THIRTEEN

Aftermarketing with the Columbia River Girl Scout Council

How do you translate the concept of aftermarketing into a series of specific steps that encourage your donors to see you as the priority? In early 1994, the Columbia River Girl Scout Council decided to concentrate on strengthening its ties with first-time and renewing donors rather than relying on an acquisition focus.

The goals were:

- to adequately thank each donor in a timely and personal manner;

- to learn more about each donor including demographics, psychographics, and communication preferences;

- to encourage donors to renew within a 45-day period;

- to encourage donors to upgrade using monthly giving.

To accomplish these goals, the Council developed a multi-step aftermarketing strategy, which is summarized herewith:

Aftermarketing Strategy

MATRIX A: All Donors' First Gifts in Fiscal Year*

First Gift of Year	Within 48 hours	In 7 days	In 15 days	In 30 days	In 45 days
Under $100					
	"Thank you" letter with donor survey	"Thank you" phone call made by development director or associate	Leadership Society invitation	If no gift: Tribute Mailer (see Matrix B if a gift is made)	If no gift: return to general database for contact in six months
$100 + Donors					
	"Thank you" letter with Leadership Society Donor member packet	"Thank you" phone call from executive director or board chair TRY TO SET APPOINTMENT FOR GIFTS OVER $250	Welcome Packet - Survey - Fact sheet - Magazine or annual report - Business cards	Partnership (monthly giving) invitation	If no gift: Tribute mailer (see Matrix B if a gift is made)

*All donors are added to newsletter/magazine subscriber list.

MATRIX B: Renewing Donors Within Year

Additional Gift Within Year	Within 48 hours	In 7 days	In 15 days	In 30 days	In 45 days
NON-LEADERSHIP SOCIETY MEMBERS					
Total under $100	"Thank you" letter with reminder of Leadership Society invitation	"Thank you" phone call by executive director or board chair	Welcome Packet - Survey (if not already returned) - Fact sheet - Currents or annual report - Tribute gift form	Partnership (monthly giving) invitation	If no gift: return to database for telephone contact within 3 months
Total of $100+	"Thank you" letter with Leadership Society member packet	"Thank you" phone call by Executive Director or Board Chair TRY TO SET APPT. FOR GIFTS OVER $250	Welcome Packet - Survey (if not already returned) - Fact sheet - Newsletter or annual report - Tribute gift form	Partnership (monthly giving) invitation	If no gift: return to database for telephone contact within 3 months
LEADERSHIP SOCIETY MEMBERS	"Thank you" letter with upgraded membership if appropriate	"Thank you" phone call by executive director or board chair TRY TO SET APPT. FOR GIFTS OVER $250	Partnership (monthly giving) invitation	Follow-up phone call by development director	If no gift: return to database for contact in 3 months

MATRIX C: Multiple Donor (Pledge) Within Year

Multiple Donor	Within 48 hours	Sent in 7 days	Sent in 15 days of pledge due for first payment	Sent in 15 days after pledge received
All	"Thank you" call from executive director or board chair	"Thank you" letter	Pledge payment request "Thank you" letter	Bank draft invitation

A key element in the aftermarketing strategy is developing a donor survey that encourages contributors to interact with the Council. The following pages contain the accompanying letter and survey.

DATE

NAME
ADDRESS
CITY, STATE ZIP

DEAR :

Your support is truly appreciated. We know you receive appeals from many worthwhile organizations and must carefully decide your priorities. We are honored you have chosen to make a gift to Columbia River Girl Scouts.

Today, more than ever, girls ages 5 through 17 confront the pressures of a changing world. Statistics cite the rising numbers of divorced or separated families, substance abusers at younger-than-ever ages, teenage pregnancies, children's suicides, and other ills.

The mission of the Girl Scouts—to help girls develop to their fullest potential and become competent, resourceful women—is as vital today as it was in 1912, when Juliette Gordon Low founded our organization. Daisy, as she was known to family and friends, firmly believed that "A girl can be anything she wants to be!" She felt that as a group, girls could share ideas and visions, seek ways to solve human problems, and enrich their lives—and the lives of others—in the process.

Your commitment to Girl Scouting—as a volunteer, an adult member, the parent of a girl member, and a financial contributor *all* make a difference.

Once again, thank you for your support! I look forward to working with you to create an environment that best serves girls and young women in Northwest Oregon and Southwest Washington.

Yours in Girl Scouting,

Wende Wilson
Executive Director

P.S. We would like to invite you to share your thoughts and concerns about girls and Girl Scouting with your Council. You and your views are important to all of us at the Columbia River Girl Scout Council. So we can better respond to your concerns, please take a minute right now to complete and return the enclosed survey. Thank you!

Columbia River Girl Scout Council Survey

Please answer the following survey questions to acquaint us with yourself and your concerns. The survey is divided into three short sections and should only take you a few moments to complete. <u>The survey is optional and your answers are strictly confidential</u>.

☐ Ms.   ☐ Mrs.   ☐ Miss_____

Address_____

City/State/Zip_____

Telephone (Daytime) _____ (Evening) _____

1 **Please indicate which of our goals are of interest to you** (check all that apply).

☐ To encourage girls from all segments of American life to develop their potential

☐ To enable girls to make friends in a safe, supportive environment

☐ To teach girls to have fun learning to become a vital contributing part of their communities

☐ To help girls live successfully in a global society

☐ To demonstrate to girls they can be all they want to be

☐ To inspire girls with the highest ideals of character, conduct, patriotism, and service

2 **Please let us know how important each one of our main programs is to you.**

Programs that build self-esteem and provide role models: We build math and science competency through troop activities, interaction with alumnae, and partnerships with OMSI and Portland State University.

     ☐ *Very important*   ☐ *Somewhat important*   ☐ *Not important*

Programs that encourage health and fitness: Emphasizing parental involvement and support, we offer day and residential camping and physical activities that promote confidence, as well as sound nutritional programs in cooperation with the American Heart Association.

☐ *Very important*   ☐ *Somewhat important*   ☐ *Not important*

Bridging the barriers that keep us from serving and being served by a pluralistic society: The Council provides a variety of outreach programs and activities that address special interests of African American, Hispanic, Native American, and Asian American girls (drill team, double dutch jump rope, swimming), provide summer and after-school activities to at-risk girls in Rose City-Columbia Housing, Pantera, Pettygrove Houses, and Klutzer Hall, and work with the migrant community in Hillsboro-Parkdale through Headstart.

☐ *Very important*   ☐ *Somewhat important*   ☐ *Not important*

Community Service: Yearly, Columbia River Girl Scouts provides 75,000 hours of community service including Christmas tree, plastics, and phone book recycling, and activities to provide food and shelter to the homeless and disadvantaged.

☐ *Very important*   ☐ *Somewhat important*   ☐ *Not important*

3 Please Tell Us About You

- Birthdate _____ - _____ - _____

- Education (please check only one)
  - ☐ Graduate or professional degree
  - ☐ College graduate
  - ☐ Some college
  - ☐ High school graduate
  - ☐ Elementary and/or some high school

- Occupation
  Title _____
  Company _____
  Address _____
  City/State/Zip _____
  Phone _____

- Were you a girl scout? ☐ YES

- Were you ever a GS volunteer?
  ☐ YES:

- Do you have a special memory of Girl Scouting? Please share it with us:

_____

_____

_____

- Other Girl Scout Alumnae in your family:
  Name _____
  Address_____
  City/State/Zip_____
  Phone
  (day)_____
  (evening)_____
  Relationship_____

  Name _____
  Address _____
  City/State/Zip_____
  Phone
  (day) _____
  (evening) _____
  Relationship _____

- I'd like to receive information on:
  □ Volunteer opportunities
  □ Adult membership
  □ Girl membership
  □ Other_____

- Areas of interest, hobbies, etc. you might share with Girl Scouts_____

  _____

- Would you prefer we communicate by
  □ Visits   □ Phone   □ Mail

□ Monthly   □ Quarterly
□ Once a Year

. . . and Your Household

- Partner's name, if appropriate:

  _____

- Occupation
  Title _____
  Company _____
  Address _____
  City/State/Zip _____
  Phone _____

- Number of children in household ____

  Name_____ Age____
  If Female, Girl Scout?
  □ Current   □ Past   □ Never

  Name_____ Age____
  If Female, Girl Scout?
  □ Current   □ Past   □ Never

  Name_____ Age____
  If Female, Girl Scout?
  □ Current   □ Past   □ Never

- Household Income
  □ $100,000 or more
  □ $75,000 - 99,999
  □ $50,000 - 74,999
  □ $30,000 - 49,999
  □ $20,000 - 29,999
  □ under $20,000

If you have any questions, comments, or suggestions, please use this space or call us at (503)620-4567 or (800)338-5248:

_____

_____

_____

_____

_____

_____

_____

_____

_____

_____

_____

Thank you for your support! It is sincerely appreciated.

CHAPTER FOURTEEN

UNICEF: Renewal and Upgrading

THE U.S. COMMITTEE for UNICEF creates a strong bond with the donor from the moment he or she makes his or her first gift. This case example is a narrative of my own experience as a new donor to the organization.

Nineteen ninety-two was a good year for our family. In December there was some extra income to spend on discretionary purchases. As a family, we decided to make some end-of-year gifts. Like many families headed by Boomers, I asked my children to help me decide our priorities: my Boomlet daughter, Cassie—then nine years old—asked that we choose charities providing services to children in drought-plagued Somalia.

POINT: Boomers tend to defer to the choices of the generations on either side of them. In this case, our charitable giving was directed by the younger generation that tends to see the whole world as their "friends."

Like many upper-middle-class families, we had received many appeals over the last few months of the year. Checking through a shoebox full of direct mail, we rapidly sorted out the organizations that addressed our objective. We sent out modest gifts to four charities: a European-based relief agency, a local medical team, a traditional children's charity, and a religious (not our own) organization. All had provided appeals regarding Somalia.

POINT: Boomers and younger audiences tend to look for charities that address their concerns, not necessarily limiting their giving to the charities they know.

Each charity received a first gift of $25. One organization never sent a thank-you letter. It turned out their policy (to keep administrative costs low) was not to acknowledge any gifts of less than $50. They made me feel unimportant and I never made a second gift. Two organizations sent thank yous—clearly form letters. Each included second envelopes asking for additional gifts right away. I was insulted by these organizations who seemed to imply I hadn't done enough.

POINT: In making their first gifts, younger audiences will tend to "test" you with an entry-level gift. If they don't like the response—too impersonal, too greedy—they won't give again.

The last organization, the U.S. Committee for UNICEF, sent a "personal" letter. It indicated that as far as they could tell, this was my first gift to UNICEF. The letter acknowledged that "not everyone chooses to give to UNICEF" and that I was "special." The letter closed with a P.S., letting me know my "New Donor" packet was on the way.

POINT: In a simple manner, UNICEF let me know they knew who I was. They moved to continue a dialogue without overloading me at the first step.

One week later, an oversized envelope arrived—emblazoned with "URGENT: New Donor Information" in red. Upon opening it, I found a letter of welcome (restating my importance to the organization), a fact sheet on UNICEF, and some phone numbers I could use in case I had questions.

POINT: The New Donor packet reinforced my feeling of importance to the organization. It also provided useful information, further educating me on UNICEF.

When I received a simple #10 envelope from UNICEF the following week, I opened it immediately. The letter acknowledged I had just made a gift but asked that, *if I were one of a very special group willing to make a second gift now,* I consider doing so. I sent another check for $25.

POINT: UNICEF wasn't expecting everyone to respond to this second appeal. They were honest in pointing this out, using it as an opportunity to find the smaller number of willing-to-renew-immediately donors.

A thank you arrived promptly. And, again, it was a "personal" letter—acknowledging that I was truly special. Not only was I a new donor, but one willing to give again in a very short period of time. Again, no attempt was made to get a further gift by enclosing an envelope.

POINT: The segmentation continued. I didn't receive the same thank-you letter I was sent for my first gift. The acknowledgment that I had made a second gift within six weeks made me feel the organization had an inkling of who I was. UNICEF didn't cheapen the gift I had just made by enclosing another envelope, which might have suggested to me that my contribution wasn't appreciated.

Within two weeks I received a closed envelope, upgraded stationery communication from UNICEF. The personalized letter suggested I might be interested in their Partnership Program and the packet contained a brochure with examples of what a significant gift to UNICEF would accomplish. I read it carefully and was delighted to discover I could provide the seeds for crops for a village for just $180 a year, payable $15 monthly.

POINT: A bargain! The monthly sum was less than the one-time gift contributions I had been writing. It was doable. I liked the project I chose to fund. It fostered independence, not dependence: another key to attracting younger adult audiences.

Another thank you. Pointing out, once more, how rare I was. Again, no envelope. This thank you was followed two weeks later by my first pledge reminder. The reminder contained an update on what was happening, in case I wanted to make a special gift as well as sending my pledge payment. At the bottom of the pledge statement form

UNICEF listed my gifts to date. A return envelope made my gift giving easy.

POINT: Even the monthly pledge statement functions as a cultivation tool for UNICEF. Seeing my gifts "grow" increased my feeling of importance and commitment.

I continued to make my pledge payments and, after the second had been acknowledged, received a special letter. UNICEF "apologized" for not being respectful of my time. Instead of requiring me to write a check each month, they were inviting me to consider making my gift via "Pledge Express"—a standing credit card authorization.

U.S. Committee for UNICEF

MONTHLY PLEDGE STATEMENT

1000H   01389385

Month:

| Amount Pledged Monthly: | Pledge Express $15.00 |

I'd like to make an extra contribution this month.
Enclosed is my check in the amount of $_____

Please make your check payable to the
U.S. Committee for UNICEF.

Your contribution is tax-deductible to the extent allowed by law.

Ms. Judith E. Nichols

ADDRESS

We also accept
☐ MasterCard   ☐ Visa   ☐ American Express

Signature

Credit Card Number   Exp. Date

Please return this upper portion with your check.

Dear Ms. Nichols,

More than 100 million landmines left over from various wars are scattered around the world. Every year, tens of thousands of people are killed or maimed by these horrible, inhumane weapons of war.

Children are the most vulnerable of all. Their natural curiosity draws them to deadly landmines. Unfortunately, too many children simply can't resist the temptation to investigate the strange objects strewn over the land of countries like Somalia, Cambodia, Mozambique, and the former Yugoslavia. Unfortunately, the outlook for children disabled by mines is bleak. In most of the 60 countries where landmines are a major problem, people are fighting for daily survival. They don't have the resources for rehabilitation programs and special schools for the disabled.

I've enclosed important information on this urgent problem. Thanks to your past generosity, we are supporting efforts to protect children from landmines, provide artificial arms and legs and rehabilitation for children injured by mines, and calling for an international effort to remove mines and ban their use. Thank you for caring for the children.

Statement of gifts received during the past 12 months

Pledge member since:
FEB-93

Month	Date	Description	Amount
OCT 94	10/20/94	Thank you for your gift by pledge express!	$15.00
SEP 94	09/20/94	Thank you for your gift by pledge express!	$15.00
AUG 94	08/22/94	Thank you for your gift by pledge express!	$15.00
JUL 94	07/20/94	Thank you for your gift by pledge express!	$15.00
JUN 94	06/20/94	Thank you for your gift by pledge express!	$15.00
MAY 94	05/18/94	Thank you for your gift by pledge express!	$15.00
APR 94	04/20/94	Thank you for your gift by pledge express!	$15.00
MAR 94	03/21/94	Thank you for your gift by pledge express!	$15.00
FEB 94	02/18/94	Thank you for your gift by pledge express!	$15.00
JAN 94	01/20/94	Thank you for your gift by pledge express!	$15.00
DEC 93	12/13/93	Thank you for your gift by pledge express!	$15.00
NOV 93	11/19/93	Thank you for your gift by pledge express!	$15.00

United States Committee for UNICEF, 333 East 38th Street, New York, NY 10016 (212) 922-2590

POINT: Boomers are much more accepting of technology than their parents. I wasn't threatened by a loss of control in accepting this option. After all, I can always cancel it!

U.S. Committee for UNICEF
Aftermarketing Timeline for
Judith E. Nichols

December '92	— UNICEF receives first gift.
December '92	— Thank you sent.
January '93	— New Donor packet sent.
January '93	— Second appeal sent, accepted.
February '93	— Thank you sent.
February '93	— Partnership Program invitation sent, accepted.
March '93	— Pledge reminder sent, pledge returned.
April '93	— Pledge reminder sent, pledge returned.
April '93	— Invitation for Pledge Express sent, returned.
May '93	— Monthly donor via VISA.

On the following page is an actual copy of the end-of-year letter I received with their annual report:

United States Committee for

United Nations Children's Fund
333 East 38th St., New York, NY 10016

ADDRESS

February 11, 1994

Ms. Judith E. Nichols

Dear Ms. Nichols,

You deserve a unique thank you.

It's wonderful that so many people respond when TV news broadcasts show live coverage of "loud" emergencies like the ongoing tragedies in the former Yugoslavia and Somalia. But it takes a special commitment to respond to the "silent" emergencies of poverty that take the lives of nearly 13 million children each year.

Your regular monthly support for the U.S. Committee for UNICEF is proof that you have that second, much more rare, kind of commitment to children.

That's why I am so glad to send your copy of the U.S. Committee for UNICEF <u>1993 Review of the Year</u>. You should take special pride in our achievements in immunizing children, providing disease-preventing sanitation and clean water, and fighting diseases like pneumonia and diarrhea.

Your generosity is helping to change the world, and for the world's poorest children I thank you very much.

Sincerely,

Hugh Downs
Chair

P.S. You are a leader in humanity's greatest quest -- a brave and ambitious attempt to make true the promise that all children should have a chance to grow healthy and strong. In 1990, the World Summit for Children set historic goals for the year 2000, including reducing malnutrition, ensuring clean water for all children, eliminating vitamin A deficiency, and eradicating polio. Your ongoing, steadfast support for the U.S. Committee for UNICEF is helping to keep this promise to children. Please continue your support in 1994 to save lives and bring a new future to children all over the world. Thanks again!

POINT: *UNICEF has continued to make me feel special.* So much so that when, in 1994, I reviewed my will, they became one of the charities I put in for a modest bequest.

CHAPTER FIFTEEN

Greenpeace Frontline:
A Committed Giving Scheme

AT THE 14TH International Fund Raising Workshop held outside of Amsterdam in October 1994, Annie Moreton of Greenpeace U.K. shared with her colleagues the example of the hugely successful Greenpeace Frontline program: a committed giving scheme. In her own words, here are the exciting details:

Greenpeace U.K. launched Greenpeace Frontline to accomplish three financial needs:

1. To increase gross annual income.

2. To generate regular, monthly income.

3. To generate long-term income (ie, not just "one off" donations, but rather donations for years to come).

We already had 250,000 current members paying an average annual membership fee of £18 (U.S.$36). So, we didn't feel we had to look outside our membership for potential donors. In addition, over 70% of our donors renew their membership each year. We felt confident there was loyalty within our existing members.

> We proposed a new membership scheme for existing Greenpeace members. The price was to be much higher than the average £18 gift per year.
>
> The scheme was to respond to members' expectations—a desire to get closer to our organization and to provide access to better quality information.

Getting Started

We surveyed our current supporters to learn how they felt about Greenpeace—whether they were interested in getting closer to the organization. We asked their opinion of several special membership schemes. Some of these options received a very positive response. We also asked how supporters would like to pay for such schemes and, more importantly, how much they would be willing to pay.

It's important for you to know that over 25% of Greenpeace memberships are paid by standing order. In the U.K., a standing order is a common way of paying bills, subscription fees, and other regular bills. You simply instruct your bank to pay a given sum from your bank account at regular intervals, usually monthly, quarterly, or yearly. The bank continues to do this until you instruct it to stop. Standing orders are easy to administer. Most importantly, once the commitment is set up you don't have to do anything—the payment is made automatically.

We were really quite surprised to find out that people generally were positive about paying by standing order. And, we were pleasantly surprised by the amounts of money people suggested paying to belong to a special membership program.

The Offer: Greenpeace Frontline

The Oxford English Dictionary defines "frontline" as "the foremost part of the field of operation; the part next to the enemy." Greenpeace *is* in the environmental front and it's our members who keep us there. So the name, Greenpeace Frontline, was a winner from the start.

Frontline would provide a priority fund for the organization. Not a reserve fund, but money to be spent on immediate campaigning priorities. A four-page letter from our executive director explained how we were developing new ways of campaigning and our need to raise additional funds to make this effective. We kept the packet very simple: the logo was the main design element. It was actually much plainer than our usual appeal mailings.

> The membership fee for Frontline is £20 (U.S.$40) each month: that's £240 (U.S.$480) per year. The fee is paid monthly, by standing order.

We offered no alternative here; no option to make a donation, to pay yearly, or to pay by check. We had identified the payment method that we thought would give us the best payback and we decided to stick with it.

In fact, when we tested giving an option to make one-off donation instead of joining Frontline, the number of people joining was *reduced* by 40%. And, when we tested asking potential members if they would join at a lower price, say £5 a month, the number of people joining Frontline was reduced by 25%.

The Benefits

The membership benefits were purposely kept low. In fact, only 2 paragraphs out of 22 mentioned what the member would receive in return for his or her commitment. This was partly because of the clear message we had received from our research: that people didn't want money "wasted" on them. But also because we were really worried about making promises we couldn't keep! The membership packet offer carefully avoided any mention of exactly what Frontline members would get and when. Instead, we emphasized that this was *their* scheme and we would develop it in response to input from its members.

Eventually, we chose two publications that already existed in Greenpeace: *Greenpeace Business* (a bi-monthly magazine produced for business and industry) and *Canonbury Post* (a single-sheet newsletter produced weekly for staff and volunteers at Greenpeace). Along with press releases, copies of detailed reports produced for specialized audiences formed the background of the benefits for supporters.

When we checked with supporters by questionnaire and telephone, we found out we were overdoing it a little. Many Frontline members simply didn't have time to read so much stuff! Now, we've stopped sending information at regular intervals. Instead we write only when there's something important to say and we try to keep the content informal. Internal notes and 10-minute audiocassettes with an update from a campaigner are much better received. And, twice a year we update Frontliners with a video. We also hold campaign briefings at the Greenpeace office.

The Results

Frontline has met our needs. We have increased our gross income, raised monthly income, and ensured that income will continue for many years, as standing-order members renew at over 90% annually.

> I estimate that Frontliners will contribute £5.5 million (U.S.$11 million) to Greenpeace over the next 10 years.

How many Frontline members have we recruited? By the spring of 1994, we had 3,500 multiplied by £240 per year: an annual income of £840,000 per year. And because Frontline membership fees are paid monthly by standing order, our finance department can rely on £70,000 arriving in our bank account each month. The finance department likes Frontline!

Adding up the cost of recruiting all our Frontline members and of providing membership benefits to them over the next 10 years gives us an income-to-cost ratio of 16 to 1.

Conclusion

Consider taking the money your organization would spend on *one* appeal mailing to your donors and, instead, spend it on launching a committed giving scheme. It will repay you over 10 years—instead of just 1.

CHAPTER SIXTEEN:

Determining Realistic, Yet Challenging, Fund-Raising Goals and Objectives

- Focus on outputs rather than inputs.

    Carefully indentify and track the smaller group of best prospects and move them along from cultivation to solicitation.

- Ask for enough money to do the job.

    Set realistic, yet challenging, goals to stretch staff and volunteers. Ask donors and prospects to commit at a meaningful level.

ONCE YOU CREATE the "organizational vision," develop a pool of committed board members and/or fund-raising volunteers, have your office of development up and running, and know your donors and prospects, you're ready to determine your fund-raising goals for each methodology your organization chooses to employ.

Not all fund-raising methodologies will do equally well. A very few will bring you spectacular gains almost effortlessly. Those are the ones to focus on, of course.

Evaluate your fund-raising methodologies using the matrix developed by the Boston Consulting Group. Growth Rate Potential and Return on Effort are its axis:

	(Very high)
RISING STAR	PROBLEM CHILD
CASH COW	DOG
	(Very low)

Growth Rate Potential

Return on Effort

(Very positive)   (Very negative)

If you don't plan carefully, you won't grow from good to great. Instead you'll only skim the surface of fund-raising gains as you're likely to go in too many directions:

- You'll miss the opportunity to focus on programs with high potential, with the result that your programs will only bring in a fraction of the potential possible. (RISING STAR)

- You'll pour unlimited effort into programs of "great potential" without determining if the results are worth it. (PROBLEM CHILD)

- Most organizations have one or two steady winners that are often ignored at their peril. (CASH COW)

- Everyone has a story about the "pet" program from hell that requires constant attention and never succeeds! (DOG)

You need to choose the best fund-raising methodologies to get the job done, not necessarily the easiest or the most comfortable.

		(Very high)
	FACE-TO-FACE	
	TELEPHONE	
SPECIAL EVENTS	DIRECT MAIL	
		(Very low)

Growth Rate Potential

Return on Effort

(Low)   (High)

Too many not-for-profits still spend a disproportionate amount of their staff and volunteer time on special-events fund raising. This is the most expensive, least productive form of fund raising for the majority of organizations. Why we do this is understandable: such fund raising is perceived as being "fun," "nonthreatening."

Although some special events have the potential for growth, few are likely to continue to bring in the dollars needed in the long run. To grow from good to great, you must be prepared to shift emphasis away from events and towards outright cultivation and solicitation.

Specifically, you should focus your development efforts on: *cultivating and soliciting major and special gifts from individuals.*

- Building a board capable and willing to take the leadership in gift-giving and gift-getting.

- Identifying and involving a small group of key major-donor prospects ($1,000-plus potential) to form the charter group of major donors and fund-raising volunteers.

- Identifying and sending grant proposals to the logical group of foundations and corporations committed to funding programs and services specific to your organization.

- Educating your constituents as to the benefits of planned gifts through your organization.

AND

Increasing unrestricted gift-giving from the broader pool of realistic prospects.

- Concentrating on renewing and upgrading the individuals with a history of giving.

- Cultivating a modest-sized, logical group of additional individuals capable of giving $100 or more annually.

(For most not-for-profits, foundation and corporate grants will bring only modest dollars for the investment of time and effort. And, most will bring in only restricted income. This may not be useful for your organization.)

How much can you grow? Many of the organizations I work with find themselves able to increase contributions by 25, 50, 100% or more *each year* once they reposition their efforts. **Set realistic, yet challenging, goals for each component of the development plan.**

Based on your organization's unique set of donors and prospects, you must determine the dollar amounts which can be raised from each methodology.

Major Giving: Face-to-Face Fund Raising

- **Board makes its own commitments before any fund raising is done to the general community**. One hundred percent of the board must give. The giving must be "meaningful" as well.

Example: ABC's board is comprised of 30 individuals. Last year, 75% gave a total of $3,700. Based on what these key volunteers are capable of giving (not their giving history to ABC!), the director of development recommends a goal of $7,500—an average gift of $250 per board member. Obviously, some board members can give more and some must give less.

Raised last fiscal year: $3,700. Goal for new fiscal year: $7,500.

- **Appointments made with past donors who have given at or above whatever level your organization defines** as **"major giving."** (For some not-for-profits this is $10,000; for others it is $100. For most, $500 to $1,000 is the norm.) Past donors should be thanked for their participation and invited to continue their support at an upgraded level. The goal should be to set face-to-face appointments with all its donors above the $1000 level.

These solicitations are the responsibility of the board. Each board member should be responsible for "giving and getting" an agreed upon amount each year. As part of their job description, board members should commit to a specific number of successful solicitations.

Example: ABC has 50 donors above $250 (exclusive of its board), with an average gift of $375. The board strategy will be to ask donors to renew and upgrade by 25%.

Raised last fiscal year: $18,500. Goal for new fiscal year: $23,125.

- **Appointments with a limited group of prospects capable of giving at or above whatever level your organization defines as "major giving."** While these solicitations can be the responsibility of the board, it often makes most sense to make this the role of the development council described in chapter five. As part of their job description, council members should commit to a specific number of successful solicitations.

Example: Prospect research has shown ABC that, on their database, there are 200 persons who are giving to other charities at the $1,000 level. For this first year, ABC decides to set a modest goal of cultivating 20 donors giving $500.

Raised last fiscal year: $—. Goal for new fiscal year: $10,000.

- **A limited group of foundations and corporations should be identified and grant proposals sent out.**

Example: ABC limits its grant writing. It decides to reapply to the 10 funders who have made grants averaging $2,500, asking for a 25% upgrade. ABC suspects that it will not have 3 of these grants renewed.

A new approach: ABC will also send out two-page letters to the top 50 corporations requesting unrestricted gifts of $500 each. The not-for-profit anticipates that 5 will respond positively.

Raised last fiscal year: $25,000. Goals for new fiscal year: $24,375. $21,875 (renewed, restricted) + $2,500 (new, unrestricted)

- **Special events that are clearly "winners" will be continued, but others are being phased out over the next three years.**

Example: ABC hosts a charity ball that has grown each year since its inception. The volunteer in charge is confident of meeting a 20% growth over the $20,000 of the previous year. Two other events will continue; goals of $10,000 and $5,000 will be the same as last year. One event which brought in only $2,000 last year was dropped.

Raised last fiscal year: $37,000. Goal for new fiscal year: $39,000.

Annual Giving

- **All supporters and past supporters (under whatever level you define as the start of major giving) should be contacted for renewal and upgrading.** A combined program of telephone and direct mail should be used for this segment, utilizing either board and volunteers as callers or a professional telecommunications service. An explanation of the direct mail/phone strategy is found in chapter 11, "Reconnecting Lapsed Donors."

Example: ABC has 1,000 donors giving under $100, with an average gift of $25. The board decides, based on its research of combined direct mail/phone programs, it will target all of its donors for which phone numbers can be found. This is 750 persons. Each will be asked to consider "making a meaningful gift" of $100, payable as $25 quarterly. It is expected that (based on the current 60% renewal rate) 450 donors will give in the new year with approximately 25% (100 individuals) upgrading to $100, 25% (100 individuals) upgrading to $50, and the remaining 250 renewing at $25.

Raised last fiscal year: $25,000. Goal for new fiscal year: $21,250.

- **A base of new supporters capable of making gifts of $100 and greater should be cultivated for first gifts**. Those donors who do not renew need to be replaced. (This is the focus of chapter nine.) Only replace with prospects capable of giving at the $100-and-greater level.

Example: With a 60% renewal rate, ABC has lost 400 donors. Fortunately, the organization has identified 2,500 "suspects"—1,500 of whom have phone numbers available—who are already on its database with the demographics of income and education, which make a gift of $100 or greater possible. It decides to use a combination of face-to-face visits and combined direct mail/phone contact to cultivate and solicit these with a goal of replacing the 400. It further assumes that 25% will, in fact, give at the $100 level; 25% will give $50; and 50% will make a "test" gift of $25.

Raised last fiscal year: $—. Goals for new fiscal year: $20,000.

- **"Wipe-up Appeals."** If budget allows, use the combined program of telephone contact and direct mail. Otherwise use personalized appeals alone—preferably hand-signed letters sent out by first-class mail.

Example: ABC projects that it will not be able to reach a significant portion of its prospect and donor base through visits and phone calls. These individuals will receive a letter explaining that ABC did try to reach them previously to ask for a gift. Just before the close of the calendar and fiscal years, ABC will also make an attempt to "reconnect" with those who declined to make a gift earlier. ABC expects it will have a pool of 2,500 names to contact: 400 past donors and 2,100 prospects. It sets a goal of connecting 40 (10%) of the donors and 100 (5%) of the prospects with an average gift of $25.

Raised last fiscal year: $—. Goal for new fiscal year: $3,500.

By looking objectively at each facet of the development program, ABC is able to grow from good to great! In fact, the organization goes from raising $109,200 to $148,750—a 36% growth in one year!

ABC's Goal-Setting in Summary:

Fund-Raising Method	Last Year's Goal	This Year's Goal
Board: Face-to-face	$3,700	$7,500
Major (renew): f-t-f	$18,500	$23,125
Major (new): f-t-f	— N/A	$10,000
Foundation/Corporate	$25,000	$24,375
Special Events	$37,000	$39,000
Annual (lapsed): Direct mail/phone contact		$21,250
Annual (replace): Direct mail/phone	— N/A	$20,000
Annual (wipe-up): Personalized mail	$25,000	$3,500
TOTALS	$109,200	$148,750

Is this unrealistic? ABSOLUTELY NOT. *Growing from good to great* is a logical outcome of following the basics of fund raising and commiting to a true aftermarketing focus.

APPENDIX A

Creating a "Wish List"

Why a Wish List?

YOU AND I know that your not-for-profit truly benefits the community. Unfortunately, your staff and volunteers are often "tongue-tied" when it comes to giving specific examples of the fine work you do. Too often, you assume others know and understand what is being accomplished and your appeals reflect this vague "doing good" stance. The Wish List gets down to specific cases and trains your staff and volunteers to articulate what your organization is all about.

The Wish List is more than a brochure. It is a training event as well. It helps to explain the link (dare I say the "synergy") between the greater program/service goal and the tangible equipment, staffing, or supplies that support that objective. It works from the bottom up to gather examples from each and every program area that highlight all programs and projects at a wide range of prices. Small and simple needs with "price tags" of under $50, as well as major gift opportunities including scholarships, building renovation, facilities namings, and endowment funding costing several thousand or million dollars are included in the final document.

Here are some examples from a Wish List I prepared for the Oregon Trail Chapter of the American Red Cross:

---

any amount — Blood Services can be contributed to the Charles Drew Scholarship Fund to train minority students entering the blood-banking field.

$5 — Blood Services tests 1 unit of blood for all transmissible diseases.

$25 — Disaster Services buys 208 Family Preparedness guides for distribution at schools, community-center meetings, and events.

$40 — Community Outreach fund a field trip or four meetings for teen girls involved with Pathways, a youth diversionary program.

$150 — Blood Services pays for the shipping costs of 100 units of red cells to support national relief efforts.

$650 — Safety and Health We need 50 "Chris Clean" mannequins to train students in first aid and CPR and meet new federal standards.

$1,000 — Community Outreach Builds classroom storage cabinets to house materials for youth education programs including Neat Kids/Safe Kids, Where I'm in Charge, Babysitting, and Basic Aid Training.

Yes, the Wish List is truly synergistic! Attractive and interesting to read, it will accomplish all of the following:

- Serve as an educational tool by explaining, by example, the fine work your organization does. At the same time, it teaches prospects that yours is a complex organization with varied (and often expensive) needs.

- Encourage upgraded annual giving by demonstrating how a slightly larger gift makes a difference. Often, modest amounts can be upgraded when suggested that . . . "$75 purchases crayons and art supplies for a class of 15 children enrolled in our after-school care program."

And, the Wish List responds to Americans' increasing receptivity to buying from catalogs and direct mail. A Simmons Market Research Bureau survey reported by the Direct Marketing Association in New York City shows that in 1990, roughly 54.4% percent of Americans shopped by mail, compared to only 24.5% percent in 1983.

- Create an enthusiasm around major and larger gifts by showing how recognition is accorded to these special donors. Naming opportunities at a variety of giving levels can be included. The Wish List is also useful in conversations with potential major-gift/planned-gift donors to identify areas of interest. (A more extensive looseleaf notebook—listing major-gift opportunities of $1,000 and greater with fuller descriptions and photographs/floorplans—can be easily prepared from the material you will have gathered.)

- Be aware of opportunities for publicity. As you get input from the staff and volunteers, unique needs will surface. These might be of interest to the media. And, if you get a donor who is willing to be spotlighted, you can use this for further publicity.

- Introduce the idea of bequest and planned giving by suggesting that, if the desire is present to make a larger than usual gift, staff can work with the prospect to make it come true.

- Acknowledge and thank volunteers by including examples of their fine work. The Wish List should include an invitation to volunteer as well—another fine synergy!

Creating a Wish List

- Choose a coordinator. This can be yourself, an outside consultant, another staff person, or a volunteer. But, it must be a person who will keep track of deadlines and encourage enthusiastic "buy-ins" from the various departments.

Either the coordinator or his or her delegate will need to:

- ■ choose a format that is attractive and cost-effective

- ■ organize the "dollar" list so you avoid duplication

- ■ create the copy that accompanies the dollar listings

- Hold a full staff meeting. The executive director must announce the Wish List concept, signaling her or his full support of the project. At this meeting, the coordinator sets follow-up meetings (typically one hour in length) with each program area. Distribute a timeline with deadlines for receiving copy, etc., and the projected date of completion of the Wish List.

- Involve as many staff, volunteers, and service users as possible in program area follow-up meetings. Help that program area to visualize what it does and how. Ask for stories, quotes, favorite photographs, and examples to illustrate the Wish List. Encourage attendees to think both small and large: You want to identify both budgeted items and "pie in the sky" possibilities.

REMEMBER: Your examples should explain what is being accomplished by holding the program and providing the service. If multiples of supplies can package a lower-priced item more attractively, include both the per-unit cost and how many (books, sets of crayons, etc.) are used in a week, month, or year.

Ideally, you will receive several examples from each program area demonstrating needs at each of the following levels:

Under $25
$26–$50
$51–$100
$101–$250
$251–$500
$501–$1,000
$1,001–$10,000
Over $10,001

- Review materials. Make sure the executive director, heads of department areas, and any other key individuals have an opportunity to review the needs lists before deciding on your format. You'll need to add in overall items, especially capital and endowment needs which may not surface from individual departments. There may also be some duplication of items which can be repackaged. (Example: three xerox machines needed for program centers in Long View, Olympia, and Woodburn.)

What format should your Wish List take? The Wish List should have a long shelf life—usually at least one to two years. It should be designed so as to avoid references that will date it.

The copy should include:

- a message from the executive director and board chair;

- an introduction to the Wish List concept;

- information on each general program and service area;

- information on volunteering;

- information on donor recognition;

- information on bequest and planned giving;

- a reply vehicle.

You can organize the Wish List by program areas or goals, if your organization is set up that way. Or, use examples from various areas throughout the copy. Arrange the brochure so that items for purchase range from the inexpensive to the expensive. (Don't move from the expensive to the inexpensive: You want prospects to step up, not down.)

The Wish List should contain numerous illustrations as well as quotations, examples, and vignettes about your organization. You may want to highlight some case examples to underscore the type of work you do and the clients you serve.

Wish List Design Tips

The Wish List is nothing more or less than a catalog. You want to motivate the reader to "buy." The first objective must be to get his or her attention.

- Visual Weight: A brief one-line headline will have more visual impact than a larger, more informative one.

    Visual elements, such as photos and headlines, on the left page receive attention from a good 80 to 100% of viewers; the right side's range is a poor 20 to 60%.

    The best spot (on a two-page spread) is the upper left corner of the left page.

    The worst spot (on a two-page spread) is the lower right corner of the right page.

- Initial Point of Focus: This is the first point on the page that is given attention. The "scanpath," or path of the eye across a page, depends on where the eye starts. If the eye begins on the right page, the left will receive less attention than if the eye started on the left page and moved to the right.

    Ideally, initial point of focus is the upper left-hand page.

- Geometry and Alignment: A reader will have a much easier time absorbing an orderly page.

    Arrange photos and accompanying headlines in a symmetrical pattern.

- The Visual Hierarchy: Organize all visual elements on a page in order of priority.

    Headlines and photos are, typically, most important and should be arranged to be read/seen first.

    Too many visual elements present problems. Don't crowd your layout. The eye stops on 12 to 17 visual elements.

- Separation: Photos and headlines should be sufficiently separated such that they are perceived as discrete visual elements. Use white space or place copy between feature photos.

SOURCE: Material adapted from *Targeted Fund Raising: Defining and Refining Your Development Strategy*, Judith E. Nichols, Precept Press, 1991

Another synergy to remember: the reply device should indicate that gifts can be made in honor or in memory of someone. Indicate that you will send a handsome announcement card to whomever the donor designates.

Try to distribute the Wish List as widely as possible. In addition to your own mailing lists, consider offering copies to the public libraries, civic groups, and local corporations, etc., to post. If you're fortunate and get initial media coverage, ask the reporter to let readers or viewers know how to request free copies.

Use the Wish List to generate new fund-raising strategies. As you start to group similar needs, new ideas for fund raising will surface. You might find logical parallels between some of your needs and various industry and professional groups. For example, your transportation Wish List items might lend themselves to a customer-oriented campaign conducted by the local automotive dealers; the money to solve your food needs could be raised by a Chef's Benefit hosted by the local restaurant association. I've had a professional advertising association raise over $200,000 for a professorship in line with their desire to honor one of their own. Because the group or industry does the fund raising on your behalf, it extends your reach.

APPENDIX B

Involving Donors and Prospects through Focus Groups

Goals for the Focus-Group Session

- To provide an opportunity for those of influence in the community to provide insights to how the organization is perceived by community leaders

- To encourage suggestions and recommendations for future directions, programs, and services that are consistent with the organization's mission

- To identify interest among those of influence in the community to work with the organization as key volunteers

---

Purpose of a Focus Group

A FOCUS GROUP is a qualitative research technique. It is a group interviewing method through which attitudes, beliefs, opinions, motivations, and reactions of people can be explored and interchanged with the aid of a trained moderator.

The focus-group technique is, by nature, exploratory. The relatively unstructured format allows for free association, question probing, and the psychological interplay of group dynamics—situations that are not possible to establish within the confines of a written questionnaire, or even one-on-one interviewing.

Although the technique offers flexibility for creating investigative situations, it follows a format and seeks a goal: that we know more after the session than before about how the organization is perceived by the community.

Focus-group sessions seldom lead to unequivocal conclusions. The results are not statistical, but interpretive. If one is aware of its limitations, the focus-group technique can be invaluable in assessing reactions, attitudes, and hypotheses to concepts, services, or products.

> The focus group is a process for gathering information, not a forum for development solutions. Keep discussion focused on *what*, rather than how, who, and when.

The focus group serves a unique function by bringing the organization face to face with the market—the real world—it seeks to involve. It provides a rapid means for gathering information in the actual language people use to describe their thoughts, ideas, and behavior.

The organization can use the focus-group interview to help it

- corroborate pre-conditioned views;
- uncover biases;
- spark creative thinking;
- develop strategies/direction.

Who is included: working with specific recommendations from the president of the organization and its executive director, the director of development should create a list of 15 to 20 persons who should be invited. They will include persons of influence and affluence. The goal is to get a cross section of

- persons not very familiar with your organization;
- representatives of the professions and activities most important to the region, including persons in banking, finance, education, medicine, military, law, agriculture, cultural organizations, religion, politics, etc.

Do not invite those already heavily involved with your not-for-profit as board members, volunteers, members, and/or donors. This includes:

- representatives from United Way;

- representatives from other not-for-profits.

How to Conduct a Focus Group

- **The facility:** Schedule the focus-group session at an easy-to-find, convenient location. The physical surroundings should have a relaxed, comfortable atmosphere, insulated from outside sounds and views. The room should be a conference room setting, with sufficient seating capacity around a table for the participants and the facilitator. Nameplates, identifying each participant and his or her affiliation, should be used.

  The respondents and facilitator should be the only persons in the focus group room. Observers are a distraction and interfere with the frankness of the discussion. During the discussion, there should be no interruptions or distractions. (Try to avoid scheduling during lunchtime; coffee, tea, and water should be available.)

- **Audiovisual equipment:** Taping the discussion will help with recall and detailed analysis. If the room does not come equipped with recording equipment, use a good-quality cassette recorder with a self-contained microphone. Be sure to have additional blank tapes and to test placing the unit for best conversation pickup.

- **Handouts:** each participant should be given a folder upon entering the room. It should contain

  - a letter of thanks from the organization's president;

  - the mission statement of the organization;

  - a list of the members of the board;

  - a summary sheet indicating the demographics of the organization: who it serves, how many, geographical outreach, programs, and services;

- a recent newsletter, favorable article, and/or brochure.

- **Role of the facilitator:** the development director, or any other designated individual, can serve as facilitator. He or she must control the group, display enthusiasm and interest for the process, and direct the discussion to its ultimate goals of (a) identifying how the organization is perceived in the community and (b) encouraging self-identification among the attendees of interest in the organization. The facilitator must encourage open discussion and elicit pertinent information without putting "words in participants' mouth." He or she directs the discussion and, at the same time, shows flexibility for the unanticipated but often highly relevant opinions to surface, encouraging full exploration of any ideas.

- **Role of organization participants:** both the president of the organization and the executive director should attend the focus group.

  - The president will welcome the participants and, in explaining her or his commitment as a volunteer, provide an affirmation of the worth of the organization.

  - The executive director will explain the organization's "vision" and answer specific questions on mission, goals, and programs/services.

  - Designate an individual to handle logistics. This person checks off participants as they arrive, directs them to seats, makes notes if requested, and is alert for any possible needs.

- **Issuing the invitations:**

  - Immediately upon identifying those to be invited, you should make a call and ask to speak with the identified participant or his or her secretary.

  - Explain that an invitation is forthcoming and ask that time be held on the participant's calendar. If it is not available, ask to be given the name of an alternate at that organization who can be invited.

- Those invited to the focus group should receive their invitations three weeks before the event. The invitation should go out over the signature of the organization president or a key volunteer with high visibility in the community. Ideally, it will go out on the company letterhead of the signee. (See sample.)

Date

Name
Address
City, State Zip

Dear (   ):

I am writing to ask you to join an intimate group of our community's leadership on (Day), (Date), (Time—Start/End)(will take one and one-quarter hours) for a very important meeting to be held at (location).

Having served as (council president, or indicate role) for (council name), I have requested its leadership to seek your advice and counsel. The purpose of this meeting is to provide the (council name) with valuable feedback on what you perceive to be our community's needs and the role that (council name) is and could play in making this a better place for all.

(assessment coordinator) will be contacting you by (date—one week in advance) to confirm your participation.

Thank you.

Sincerely,

Name
Title

A minimum of 6 participants and a maximum of 12 (outside of the facilitator, the board president, executive director, and logistics coordinator) are needed for optimum interaction. It should be assumed that many of those contacted will *not* respond.

- Ten days *after* the invitations are mailed, call the invitees. Confirm that the invitations have been received and ask for a response. Any additional follow-up should be done as necessary.

Structuring the focus-group session: the focus-group session must begin and end promptly. It should take one and one-quarter hours:

5 minutes: Welcome—Introduction of participants, organization president, turns over to executive director

5 minutes: Explains purpose of meeting, turns over to finance resource development consultant

1 hour: Starting Questions

1. When I say "type of organization (youth, medical, educational)," what do you respond?

2. When I say "XXX Organization," what do you respond?

3. Read mission statement (ask participants to follow along in handout packet) and ask for comments on its relevance.

4. Read organization demographics (ask participants to follow along in handout packet) and ask for comments.

NOTE: Because a focus-group session cannot and should not be fully structured, encourage conversation to explore all concerns/comments fully.

5 minutes: Organization president thanks participants.

Resources for Learning More about Focus Groups

FOCUS GROUPS: A Guide for Marketing and Advertising Professionals by Jane Farley Templeton

This book offers vignettes, insights into the mechanics, structure, reporting, evaluation, and interpretation of focus groups, and explains the interpersonal dynamics that operate between the moderator, clients, and participants.

THE HANDBOOK FOR FOCUS GROUP RESEARCH by Thomas L. Greenbaum

More advanced, this book explains how to select and evaluate moderators and facilities and reviews the latest technology. Greenbaum explains various techniques you can use to yield more information.

Both available from American Demographics Press, (800) 828-1133

Follow-up thank you: The coordinator should prepare letters thanking participants. They should go out over the organization president's signature the next day. If appropriate, the letters should address any specifics (e.g., request for additional information). Always invite the individual to become more involved.

Your next steps might include:

- suggesting a tour of the facility;

- extending an invitation to an upcoming program;

- providing a packet of information on a subject of interest.

APPENDIX C

Gift Stewardship and Accountability

STEWARDSHIP AND ACCOUNTABILITY are key concerns of your donors and prospects. You need to provide them with information on how you address these issues *before* they make their gifts.

Among the questions that need to be addressed:

Who can accept gifts? Does the development officer have that right? The chair of the board? Does gift acceptance require a full board/committee meeting? Gift acceptance policies will protect your organization: too often, before checking, a well-meaning volunteer tells the donor that his or her gift will be welcome. Sometimes gifts have complications. A policy that requires review by a committee provides a "cooling off" period.

What types of gifts will your organization accept? There may be a limit to what you want to handle in terms of management and stewardship. Your organization may not want any gifts of real estate or may want to accept such gifts only with the condition that such gifts of stock, real estate, and real property are put up for sale immediately. You must balance out your ability to manage long-term assets with the potential donor's needs.

How will you show your appreciation? Recognition needs to be consistent for all donors. Decide levels for namings, endowments, and other types of fund raising. Will donors receive plaques or premiums? There's a cost involved. How much is to be given back?

At what level may donors restrict their gifts? As we go further up the gift-giving ladder, the proportion of gifts that come in with restrictions increases. Very few donors of $1 million allow an organization to use their gift in any way the charity chooses. Where will you put the "breaks"?

How will you recover operating and fund-raising costs from unrestricted, restricted, and endowment gifts? There are numerous methods for recovering fund-raising costs, ranging from levying a percentage tax on all restricted gifts to using unrestricted gifts to cover costs on restricted fund raising. Once you decide on your policy, volunteers and staff must communicate this information to potential donors.

What levels of funding are required for endowments, scholarships, facility and room namings, life-income vehicles including trusts, annuities, and pooled-income funds? It needs to be consistent for all donors: you can't "sell" the same type of room to a member of the board for less than you would to the general public. And, it's important not to accept less than is needed to handle the costs involved with the endowment's payout. It's better for everyone if the rules are set out clearly, in advance.

How will you handle the possibility of immediate costs involved with an endowment gift? For example, a donor who gives you a gift of $100,000 of stock. Your financial committee decides not to sell the stock, believing the stock's value will increase substantially over the next few years. But, the donor specifies that his gift fund a scholarship of $2,000 per year beginning immediately. How will you fund this?

What about in-kind donations? Do you take all that are offered? How are they valued (internally) to the organization?

Once you've formulated the initial answers to these questions you need to create a document titled "Gift Stewardship Guidelines and Policies" which is available to all concerned. You should also consider adding a line onto all your fund-raising brochures and reply vehicles indicating you have a written policy for gift stewardship and offering to provide it upon request.

Patricia Lewis, president of the National Society of Fund Raising Executives, concurs that stewardship questions are an ethical concern. In addition to the questions I've outlined, she recommends deciding on your policy for sponsorship and cause-related marketing; your investment policies; use of paid versus commission-based fund-raising consultants; privacy of donor information issues; and reporting of pledges and planned gifts.

Your gift stewardship guidelines will expand as your fund-raising efforts grow. It's a living document that needs to be updated yearly at your board retreat to reflect the stage of your development program.

Sample Gift Stewardship and Accountability Guidelines

1. What types of gifts does ABC organization accept?

The ABC Organization accepts gifts of cash, securities, irrevocable planned-gift arrangements utilizing bequests, life insurance, trusts and annuities, as well as in-kind and real-property contributions.

- Stock gifts are attributed the median price on the day received.

- Gifts of real property valued at $5,000 and over should be evaluated by an independent appraiser. The ABC Organization does not assign a value for tax purposes to non-cash contributions, although it will assign a general "internal" level for donor recognition.

- Pledges paid within a five-year period are assigned full, current value. Until they are "paid in full," they are considered to be "accounts receivable" and assigned 70% of value.

- Deferred gifts (including, but not limited to, annuities, unitrusts, pooled-income vehicles, and irrevocable bequests) are assigned a value, adjusted for current value using actuarial tables for the age of the donor.

- Bequests that are revocable are assigned a value of $1,000. If the actual amount is known it is recorded for an "internal" level of donor recognition only.

2. Who can accept gifts on behalf of ABC?

An outright, unrestricted cash gift of any amount may be accepted by the executive director, development staff, or members of the board.

A non-cash gift (including real property, stock, or a planned-gift vehicle) or restricted cash gifts (allowed at $1,000 or greater) may be accepted by the executive director, development staff, or members of the board subject to a review by ABC Organization's finance committee. The review will be scheduled within a 45-day period.

3. What forms of donor recognition are given?

All gifts to the ABC Organization are sincerely appreciated and promptly acknowledged with a letter.

Unless a donor requests anonymity, all contributors for the immediate past fiscal year (July 1–June 30) are listed in an Annual Report/Honor Roll of Donors.

Donors who contribute at and above $100 are considered to be members of ABC's Patron's Circle

Members	$100 to $999 annual gifts
Contributors	$1,000 to $9,999 annual gifts
Benefactors	$10,000 and above cumulative gifts
Key Club	Bequests and planned gifts

A personalized certificate of appreciation is provided to members of the Patron's Circle upon request.

For membership in the Key Club, donors must indicate, in writing, that they have included the ABC Organization or a particular department in their wills or other planned-giving vehicle. No amount need be specified.

4. How are fund-raising costs recovered from contributions?

The ABC Organization raises funds on behalf of the organization and its entities through an intensified development strategy utilizing personal solicitations, corporate and foundation proposals, direct mail, telecommunications, and special events.

- All direct costs for fund raising are recovered from these efforts before funds are distributed.

- 20% of each undesignated gift is assigned to the Office of Development to cover the costs of fund raising.

- For designated or restricted gifts, direct costs of fund raising are recovered by the following formula:

  10% levy for gifts of up to $100,000

  5% levy for gifts of over $100,000

  This levy can be "paid" in any of the following ways:

  - with donor agreement, taken from the gift

  - with donor agreement, supplementing the gift

  - with department agreement, taken from another source of revenue including unrestricted and designated funds

- After fund-raising costs are recovered, the ABC Organization will then allocate the remaining unrestricted dollars among its entities and departments. Recommendations for distribution will be made quarterly by the administrators' council.

5. What levels of funding are required for a named endowment?

$10,000 or greater establishes a named endowment fund. The first grant is made during July following completion of the first full fiscal year after the fund's establishment. The grant is limited to 5% from the interest income, with the remaining interest going back into the endowment to build principal.

6. What levels of funding are required for trusts and annuities?

$50,000 establishes a charitable remainder trust or annuity. Generally, these are made available to individuals age 55 or over. Up to 2 beneficiaries may be incorporated to receive payments. The funding of the trust or annuity must be done with a vehicle which can be readily liquidated prior to payments commencing.

7. What are the requirements for bequest gifts?

Bequest gifts of any amount are welcome. Because it is difficult to anticipate the needs of the future, donors are requested to leave their bequest gifts to ABC Organization unrestricted, or designated rather than restricted.

8. What kinds of in-kind donations are accepted?

A limited amount of office equipment, durable goods, and specific materials in good condition is needed. In-kind gifts are assigned no value by the ABC Organization. It is the responsibility of the donor to do so for tax purposes.

9. What is ABC Organization's policy for sponsorship and cause-related marketing? For premiums and incentives?

ABC Organization recognizes that its name carries weight in our community. Before agreeing to lend its implied endorsement to a for-profit entity through sponsorship and/or cause-related marketing, the sponsorship committee will meet, review the request, and advise the board. A decision will be rendered within 45 days of the request.

Fund-raising appeals which, in exchange for a contribution, offer premiums or incentives (the value of which is not insubstantial, but which is significant in relation to the amount of the donation) will advise the donor of the fair market value of the premium or incentive and that the value is not tax deductible.

10. What are ABC Organization's investment policies?

As an ethical, responsible member of our community, ABC Organization will not invest in stock/bond vehicles that either directly or indirectly refute our mission. These include: tobacco, drug and alcohol products, as well as companies with a history of discriminating by race/ethnicity, age, gender, or sexual orientation. We do not do business with countries that ignore the civil rights of their citizens.

11. What is ABC Organization's stance on the use of paid versus commission-based fund-raising consultants?

ABC subscribes to the principles of both the American Association of Fund-Raising Counsel and the National Society of Fund Raising Executives. We do not hire fund raisers on a percentage basis.

12. What is ABC Organization's stance on privacy of donor information issues?

ABC recognizes that donors are at the heart of our organization's viability and that we have strong responsibilities to protect their privacy.

- All donors are contacted prior to the printing of the annual Honor Roll in the September issue of our newsletter and advised that names are being listed. Donors are given the option of remaining anonymous.

- Donors are welcome to request and receive a complete copy of any written materials being held in their file.

- Only authorized staff and board members may view a donor file.

- Donor files remain on-site.

SOURCE: expanded from *Targeted Fund Raising: Defining and Refining Your Development Strategy*, Judith E. Nichols, Precept Press, 1991

APPENDIX D

Creating a Timeline for Implementation

O**FTEN, THE GREATEST** difficulty an organization has is in making sure that the agreed-upon fund-raising methodologies proceed on schedule.

If possible, conduct your development audit well in advance of the new fiscal year. By doing so, you will have time to create a realistic timeline. It will take at least three months to complete the organizational steps recommended on the following page. Some, like the Wish List and Matching Gift brochure, are not urgent at the beginning. However, they will quickly be needed. It's better to delay the actual fund-raising steps until your organizational steps are well in hand.

Overall Goals

Organizational Steps:

- Restructuring the office of development to support goals and objectives, including staffing and computerization.

- Developing a key group of volunteers for fund raising at the major-gifts level.

- Creating and adopting gift stewardship and accountability guidelines.

- Creating a structure for the Leadership Society Gift Club as well as supporting materials.

- Creating an aftermarketing matrix for renewing and upgrading donors, including letters of appreciation and acknowledgment.

- Creating an ongoing structure for prospect research and identification.

- Creating supporting fund-raising materials including business reply envelopes and inquiry cards, a mission statement piece, a brochure for corporate and foundation approaches, a Wish List, a Matching Gifts brochure, and a tribute gift flyer.

Once the overall development strategy is agreed upon, the specific fund-raising action steps can be defined and a timeline for implementation is needed. A timeline for the next two to three years should be prepared.

The timeline must take into account a number of factors:

- Making a realistic assessment of the time demands on the board, executive director, development director and staff for non-fund-raising assignments.

- The impact of other not-for-profits' fund raising (including United Way) on timing of solicitations and events.

- Providing a steady and logical flow of information that moves the cycle of cultivation, solicitation, and acknowledgment along.

Fund-Raising Steps:

- Annual Giving for Operational Needs: Fund raising should focus on using a combined direct mail/phone program to contact as many current donors as possible, requesting renewed and upgraded gifts.

- Major Giving for Capital Needs: Face-to-face cultivation and solicitation by volunteers and staff.

- Planned Giving for Endowment Needs: Cultivation via a quarterly newsletter, ads in communication vehicles, inquiry cards. Initial appointments with first group of prospects.

- Impact of other not-for-profits' fund raising (including United Way) on timing of solicitations and events.

- Providing a steady and logical flow of information to the prospect that moves the cycle of cultivation, solicitation, and acknowledgment steadily along.

Once the strategy is agreed upon, a timeline for implementation should be developed. The timeline should be a flexible planning document that is expanded, corrected, and modified with opportunities. It reflects what is happening and what will happen. It forms the basis of your planning for the next fiscal year. A well-thought-out timeline will enable your organization to plan logically for both expenses and income and is an essential tool in evaluating how well the development program is doing when compared to agreed-upon expectations.

The sample timeline presented on the following pages is a beginning outline of what could be done to move a development program along. Each month, refinements are added to indicate what has been accomplished in the previous month, and to be more specific about what will be happening in the immediate months ahead.

Proposed Timeline

The sample timeline that follows assumes that the organization has completed its organizational steps and implements its revised development strategy just before the start of a new fiscal year.

Remember to allow time for the preliminary steps!

    1. (2–6 months)   Audit conducted and adopted

    2. (2–6 months)   Organizational steps completed

Each month, the steps outlined in the aftermarketing matrix for acknowledgment and appreciation must be the priority. In addition:

Month 1 (New Fiscal Year)

- Board fund-raising retreat*

  - Kick off board campaign with goal of l00% participation at a meaningful level. Completion: (1 month hence)

  - Review audit strategy, board fund-raising role

- Review of gift stewardship/accountability guidelines including donor acknowledgment

- Send out thank-you letters to previous year's supporters indicating they will be acknowledged in honor roll and asking for early support in new fiscal year.

* This organization has made the decision that the board, not a development council, will handle all major gift cultivations and solicitations. If your organization decides to use a development council, trainings and gift giving by the board and council can occur simultaneously in the first month.

Month 2

- Campaign Fiscal Year XXXX

  - Kick off staff campaign with goal of 100% participation at a meaningful level. Completion: (1 month hence)

  - Initial board assignments made

- Direct Mail/Phone Campaign to previous fiscal year donors

  - Volunteer callers recruited

  - Materials prepared (Pre-approach letter, script, tracking)

Month 3

- Campaign Fiscal Year XXXX

  - Kick off volunteer campaign with goal of 100% participation at a meaningful level. Completion: (1 month hence)

- Direct Mail/Phone Campaign to previous fiscal year donors

  - Pre-approach letters sent

- Begin monthly mailings of pinpointed educational appeals to prospects

Month 4

- Campaign Fiscal Year XXX—Kick-Off Meeting

  - Gift commitments confirmed from all board members

  - Assignments confirmed

  - Training held

  - First group of prospect appointments begin

- Direct Mail/Phone Campaign to previous fiscal year donors

  - Phone calls made

- Monthly mailings of pinpointed educational appeals to prospects (which asks for gifts above $100)

Month 5

- Campaign Fiscal Year XXXX appointments continue
- Direct Mail/Phone Campaign to previous fiscal year donors
  - Phone Calls completed; letters sent to those not reached
- Monthly mailings of pinpointed educational appeals to prospects

Month 6

- Half-year analysis prepared
- Campaign Fiscal Year XXXX appointments continue
- Monthly mailings of pinpointed educational appeals to prospects
- Invitational mailing of planned-giving newsletter

Month 7

- Board fund-raising training retreat
- Campaign Fiscal Year XXXX appointments continue
- Follow up on planned-giving inquiries

Month 8

- Campaign Fiscal Year XXXX appointments continue
- Direct Mail/Phone Campaign to acquisition prospects of $100 and above
  - Volunteer callers recruited
  - Materials prepared (pre-approach letter, script, tracking)
- Monthly mailings of pinpointed educational appeals to prospects

Month 9

- Campaign Fiscal Year XXXX appointments continue
- Second issue, planned-giving newsletter
- Preparation of proposed next fiscal year development budget
- Direct Mail/Phone Campaign to acquisition prospects of $100 and above
  - Pre-approach letters sent

Month 10

- Work with board chairman to create structure for the new fiscal year board campaign
- Direct Mail/Phone Campaign to acquisition prospects of $100 and above
  - Phone calls made

Month 11

- Campaign Fiscal Year XXXX appointments continue
- Campaign Fiscal Year XXXX+1 begins
  - Present plans to board
  - Begin new fiscal year board campaign
- End of year direct mail wrap-up appeal created
- Begin to create newsletter/annual report format

Month 12

- Campaign Fiscal Year XXXX appointments conclude
- Campaign Fiscal Year XXXX+1
  - Begin new fiscal year staff campaign
- Third issue, planned-giving newsletter
- End of year direct mail wrap-up appeal mails

NOTE: A holiday direct-mail appeal can be added in December and a tribute/memorial appeal in May if desired.

Bibliography

I drew upon a variety of resources in my research. Here is a sampling of those publications and organizations I found especially helpful.

Sources for General Demographic and Psychographic Information Applicable to Not-for-Profits and Fund Raising

American Demographics
    P.O. Box 68
    Ithaca, New York 14851
    (800) 828-1133

GREY INSIGHTS newsletter (free on request)
    Grey Advertising Inc.
    777 Third Avenue
    New York, NY 10017
    (212) 546-2000

Roper's *The Public Pulse*
    205 East 42nd Street
    New York, NY 10017
    (212) 599-0700

Research Alert
    37-06 30th Avenue
    Long Island City, NY 11103
    (718) 626-3356

Highly Recommended for
Donor-Focused Marketing

*AFTERMARKETING: How to Keep Customers for Life through
        Relationship Marketing*
Terry G. Vavra
Irwin 1992

BEYOND MAXI-MARKETING
Stan Rapp and Thomas L. Collins
McGraw Hill 1994

*BUILDING CUSTOMER LOYALTY: How You Can Help Keep
        Customers Returning*
Barbara A. Glanz
Irwin 1994

*GUERRILLA MARKETING EXCELLENCE: The Fifty Golden Rules
        for Small-Business Success*
Jay Conrad Levinson
Houghton Mifflin 1993

HOW TO WIN CUSTOMERS AND KEEP THEM FOR LIFE
Michael LeBoeuf, Ph.D.
G.P. Putnam's Sons 1987

*KEEPING CLIENTS SATISFIED: Make Your Service Business More
        Successful and Profitable*
Robert W. Bly
Prentice Hall 1993

MANAGING KNOCK YOUR SOCKS OFF SERVICE
Chip R. Bell and Ron Zemke
AMACON 1992

PERSONALITY SELLING: Selling the Way Customers Want to Buy
Tom Anastasi
Sterling 1992

POWER MARKETING FOR SMALL BUSINESS
Jody Hornor
The Oasis Press/PSI Research 1993

RAVING FANS: A Revolutionary Approach to Customer Service
Ken Blanchard and Sheldon Bowles
William Morrow & Co. 1992

*RELATIONSHIP MARKETING: Successful Strategies for the Age of
    the Customer*
Regis McKenna
Addison Wesley 1991

*SATISFACTION GUARANTEED: 236 Ideas to Make Your Customers
    Feel Like a Million Dollars*
Byrd Baggett
Rutledge Hill Press 1994

SPIN SELLING
Neil Rackham
McGraw Hill 1988

SUCCESSFUL DIRECT MARKETING METHODS
Bob Stone
NTC Business Books 1994

THE NEW HOW TO ADVERTISE
Kenneth Roman and Jane Maas
St. Martin's Press 1992

*THE ONE TO ONE FUTURE: Building Relationships One Customer
    at a Time*
Don Peppers and Martha Rogers, Ph.D.
Currency/Doubleday 1993

*UPSIDE-DOWN MARKETING: Turning Your Ex-Customers into
    Your Best Customers*
George R. Walther
McGraw Hill 1994

Highly Recommended For
Demographic and Psychographic
Information

AGEWAVE
Ken Dychtwald with Joe Flower
Tarcher 1988

BEYOND MIND GAMES: The Marketing Power of Psychographics
Rebecca Piirto
American Demographics Books 1991

*CAPTURING CUSTOMERS: How to Target the Hottest Markets of
    the' 90s*
Peter Francese and Rebecca Piirto
American Demographics Books 1991

FUTURE TENSE: The Business Realities of the Next Ten Years
Ian Morrison and Greg Schmid
William Morrow & Co. 1994

*GENDERFLEX: Men & Women Speaking Each Other's Language at
    Work*
Judith C. Tingley, Ph.D.
AMACOM 1994

GENERATIONS: The History of America's Future, 1584 to 2069
William Strauss and Neil Howe
William Morrow & Co. 1991

GREAT EXPECTATIONS: America and the Baby Boom Generation
Landon Y. Jones
Ballantine 1980

MARKETING TO BOOMERS AND BEYOND
David B. Wolfe
McGraw Hill 1993

MARKETING TO AND THROUGH KIDS
  Selina S. Guber and Jon Berry
  McGraw Hill 1993

MARKETING TO THE AFFLUENT, SELLING TO THE AFFLUENT,
  NETWORKING WITH THE AFFLUENT
  Dr. Thomas J. Stanley
  Irwin 1988

MARKET OWNERSHIP: The Art & Science of Becoming #1
  William A. Sherden
  AMACOM 1994

MARKET SEGMENTATION: Using Demographics, Psychographics
  and Other Niche Marketing Techniques to Predict Customer
  Behavior
  Art Weinstein
  Probus 1994

RELATIONSHIP FUNDRAISING
  Ken Burnett
  White Lion Press (UK) 1992

SEGMENTING THE WOMEN'S MARKET: Using Niche Marketing to
  Understand and Meet the Diverse Needs of Today's Most
  Dynamic Consumer Market
  E. Janice Leeming and Cynthia F. Tripp
  Probus 1994

SELLING THE STORY: The Layman's Guide to Collecting and
  Communicating Demographic Information
  William Dunn
  American Demographics Books 1992

TARGETING THE NEW PROFESSIONAL WOMAN
  Gerry Myers
  Probus 1994

THE AFFLUENCE INDEX, 1992-93 Edition
  Concert Music Network
  271 Madison Avenue
  New York, NY 10016
  (212) 532-1900

THE BARNA REPORT, 1992-93
  George Barna
  Regal Books 1992

THE LIFESTYLE ODYSSEY
  Editors of *Research Alert*
  Sourcebooks 1992

*THE AFFLUENCE EXPLOSION: The Real Affluents, The Real
    Impact*
  Compiled by Alert Publishing, Inc., 1990
  37-06 30th Avenue
  Long Island City, NY 11103
  (718) 626-3356

*THE MASTER TREND: How the Baby Boom Generation is Remaking
    America*
  Cheryl Russell
  Plenum Press 1993

*THE SEASONS OF BUSINESS: The Marketer's Guide to Consumer
    Behavior*
  Judith Waldrop with Marcia Mogelonsky
  American Demographics Books 1992

WHO WE ARE: A Portrait of America
  Sam Roberts
  Times Books 1993

Sources for Demographic
and Psychographic Information
Directly Pertinent to Not-for-Profits

Giving and Volunteering in the United States
Independent Sector
1828 L Street, NW, Suite 1200
Washington, DC 20036
(202) 223-8100

Giving USA
AAFRC Trust for Philanthropy
25 West 43rd Street
New York, NY 10036
(212) 354-5799

The Mind of the Donor
Barna Research Group, Ltd.
647 West Broadway
Glendale, CA 91204
(818) 241-9300

The Chronicle of Philanthropy
1255 23rd Street, NW
Washington, DC 20037
(202) 466-1200

The Foundation Center (publishers of *The Foundation News*)
79 Fifth Avenue
New York, NY 10003
(800) 424-9836

Fund Raising Management
224 Seventh Street
Garden City, NY 11530
(516) 746-6700

The Non-Profit Times
P.O. Box 408
Hopewell, NY 08525
(609) 466-4600

Donors Magazine (devoted to the use and application of information
    technology in fund raising)
CVSS, Compton Martin
Bristol BS18 8JP United Kingdom
For a free sample copy call
(44) 0761-221810 or Fax (44) 0761-221910

About the Author

Judith E. Nichols, Ph.D., CFRE, is an Oregon-based development consultant with a variety of not-for-profit clients across the U.S. and in Canada and Europe. A popular trainer and presenter, she specializes in helping organizations understand the implications of our changing demographics and psychographics on fund raising, marketing, and membership. Dr. Nichols has been featured at numerous conferences, workshops, and symposia in the United States, Europe, and Canada.

Dr. Nichols is the editor of *Philanthropy Trends that Count*, a quarterly newsletter, and is a columnist for *Contributions*. She has been interviewed by many publications, including *The Chronicle of Philanthropy* and the *Irish Times*, and her articles have appeared in *Fund Raising Management*.

She has more than 20 years of fund raising and marketing experience, working with higher education as well as with arts and cultural, health-related, human benefit and social service, membership, and youth organizations. Clients include the American Heart Association, Girl Scouts of the USA, and the Presbyterian Church (USA) Foundation.

An NSFRE-certified senior fund raiser, Dr. Nichols served as Vice President for Development at Portland State University, Oregon, and headed an award-winning development program at Wayne State University, Detroit, and at the New Jersey Institute of Technology.

Additional books
by
JUDITH E. NICHOLS, PH.D., CFRE

Pinpointing Affluence:
Increasing Your Share of Major Donor Dollars   **$40**
     " . . . a highly informative book that can strengthen your fund-raising program by prompting you to rethink who your best donors are and redirect your efforts toward those capable and willing to give."

—The Complete Professional's Library

Targeted Fund Raising:
Defining and Refining Your Development Strategy   **$40**
     "Right on target . . . sound, practical advice on fund raising with a perceptive examination of the trends affecting individual, foundation, and corporate donors today. A lucid work, ***Targeted Fund Raising*** helps you separate the wheat from the chaff."

—Contributions

Changing Demographics:
Fund Raising in the 1990s   **$40**
     " . . . gives fund raisers a veiw of *their* destiny. Helps put the trends into a coherent perspective. It's a fascinating and enlightening review."

—CASE Currents

Judy Nichols' books are available from:

Precept Press
A Division of Bonus Books, Inc.
160 East Illinois Street
Chicago, Illinois 60611, USA
(800) 225-3775